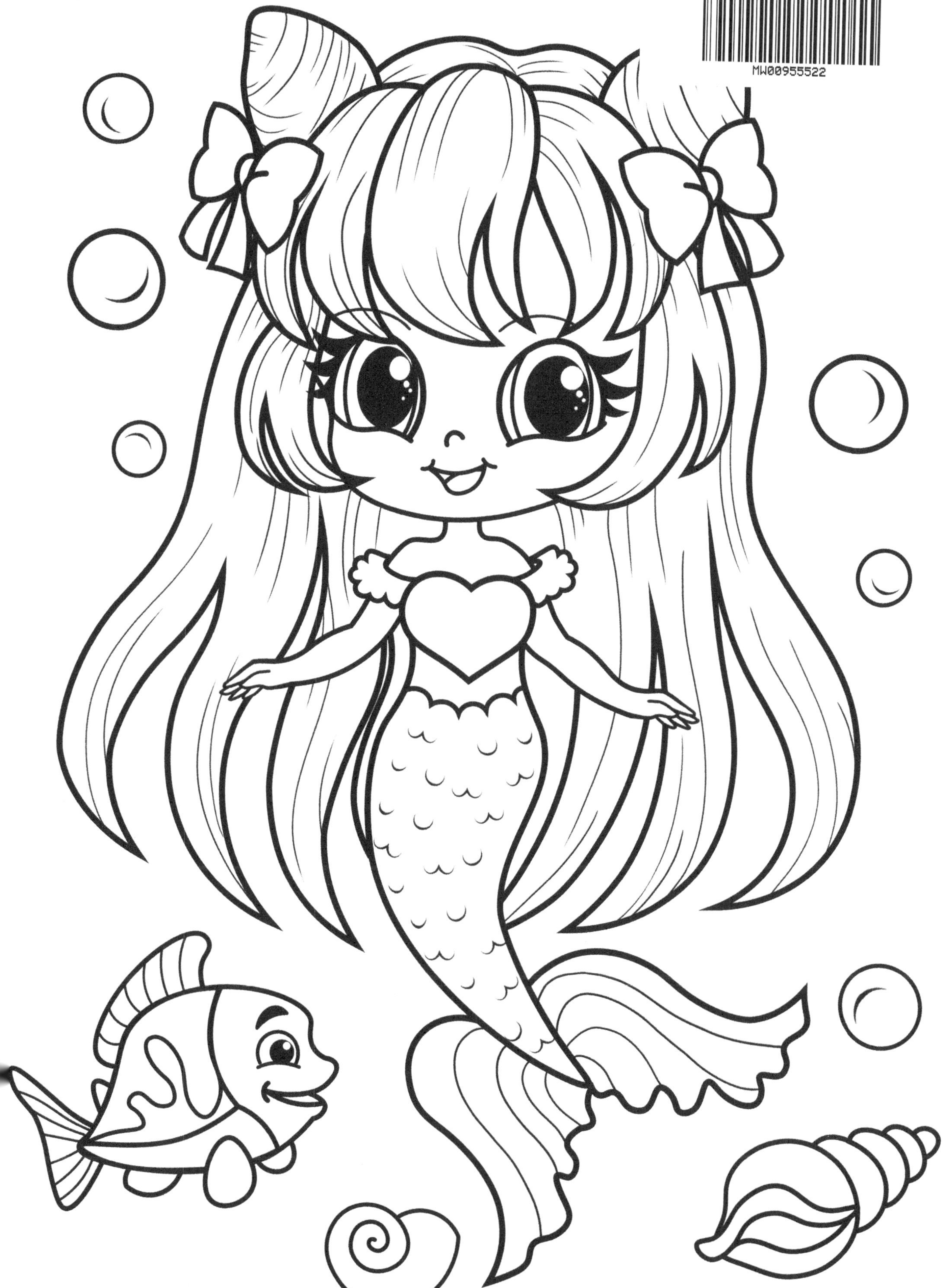

Happy Mermaids: Coloring Book For Kids Ages 4-8
ISBN: 979-8767813278
For more informations and to stay updated on new coloring books visit our web site :
www.coloringbookkim.com

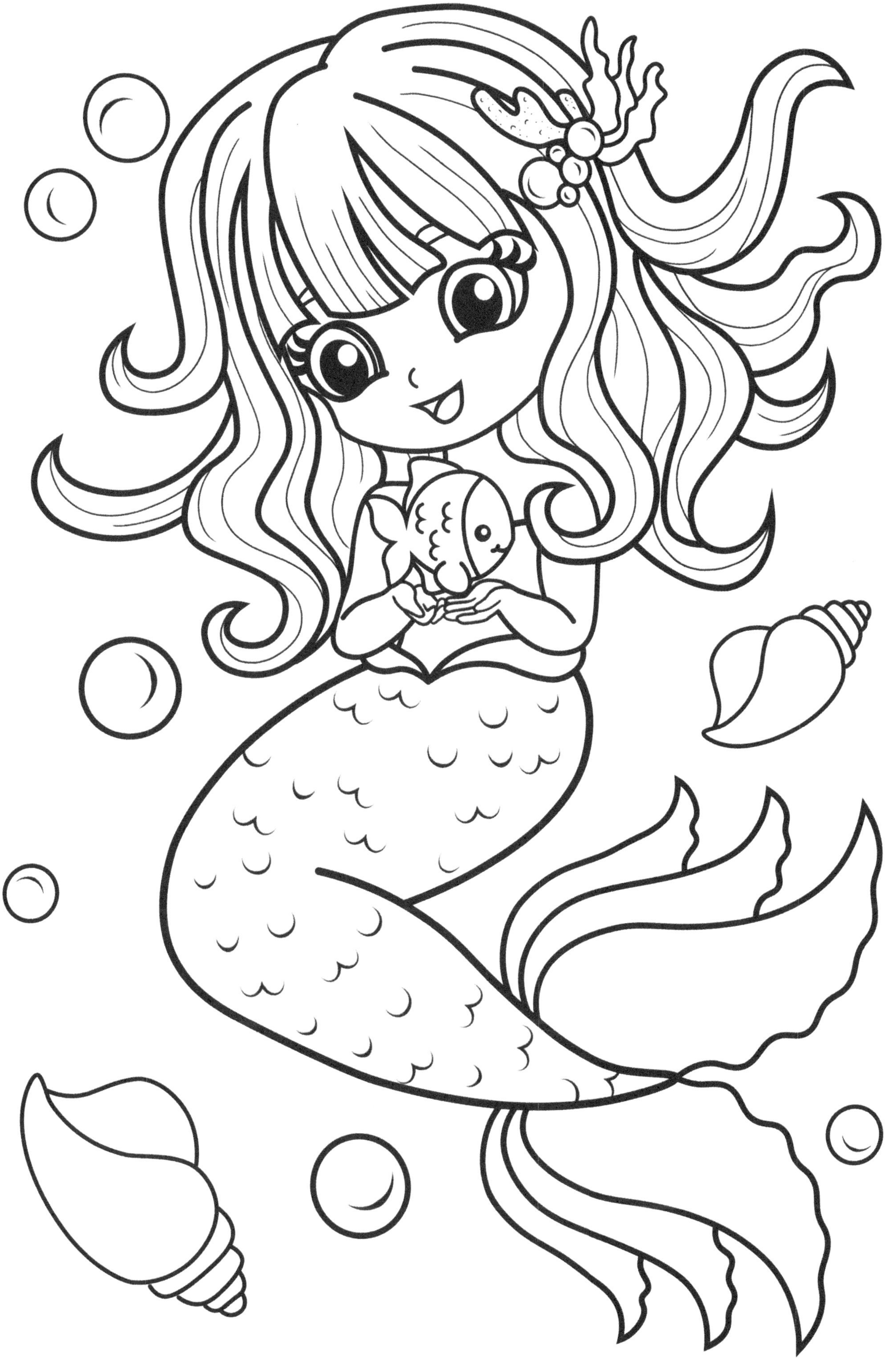

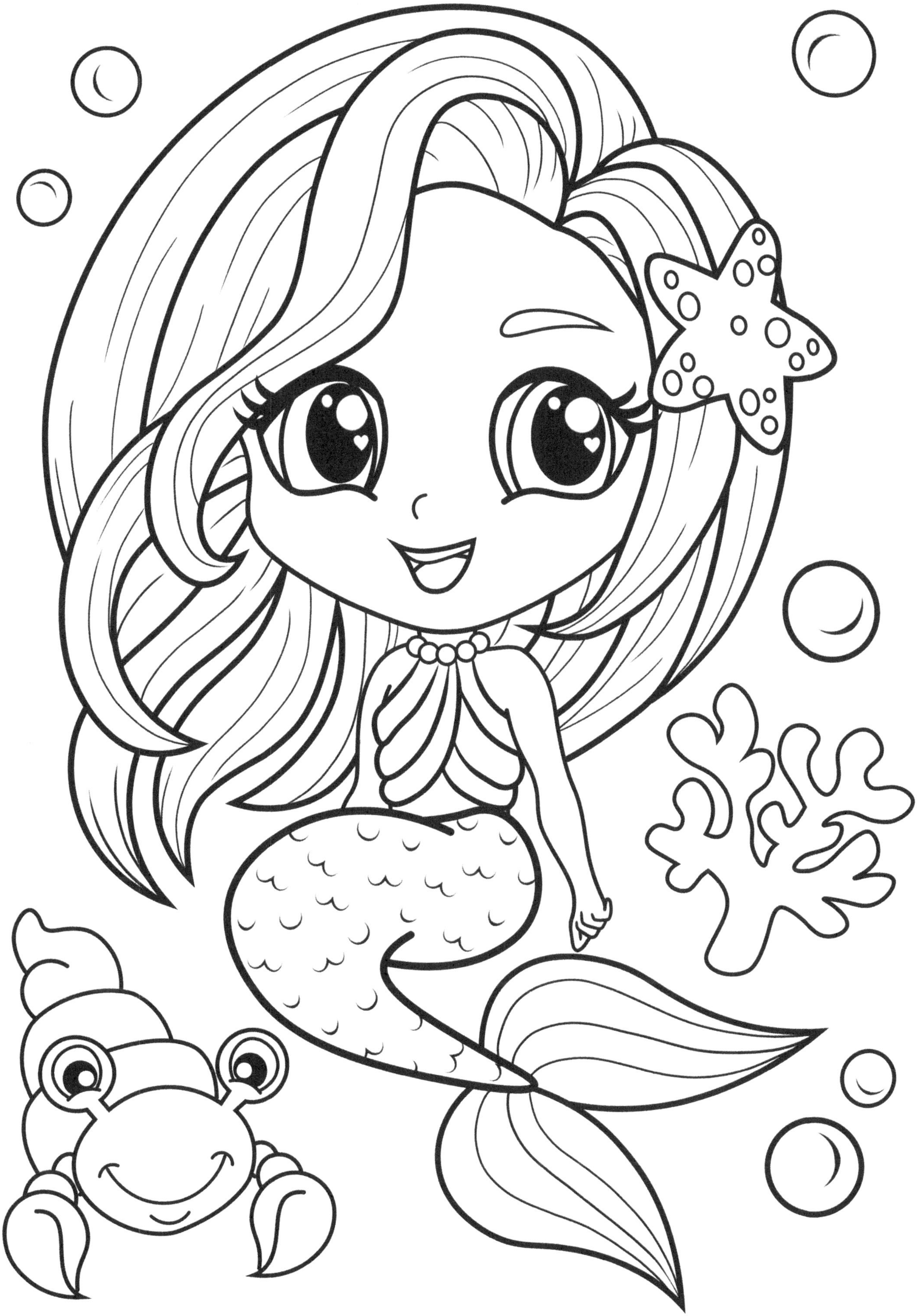

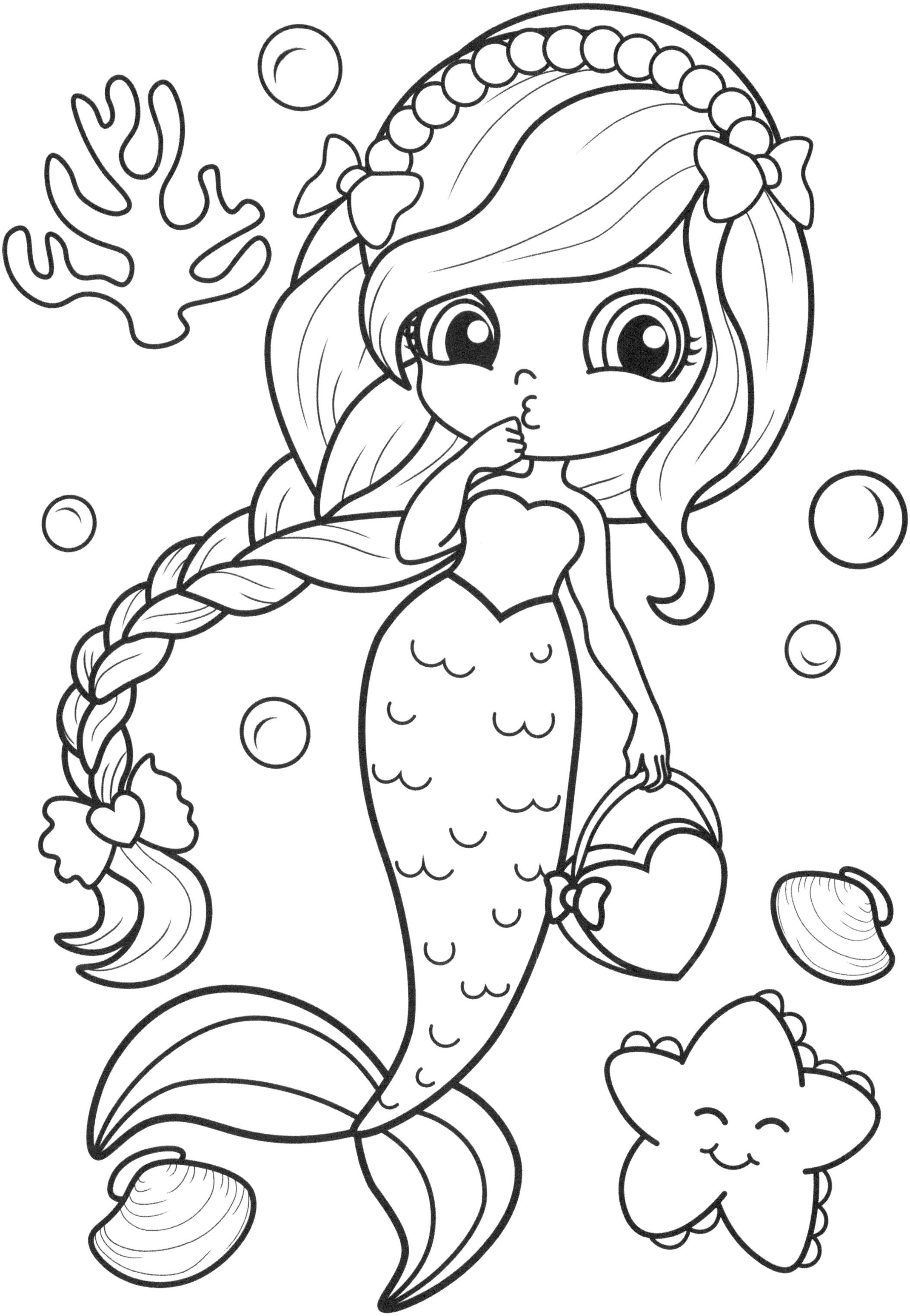

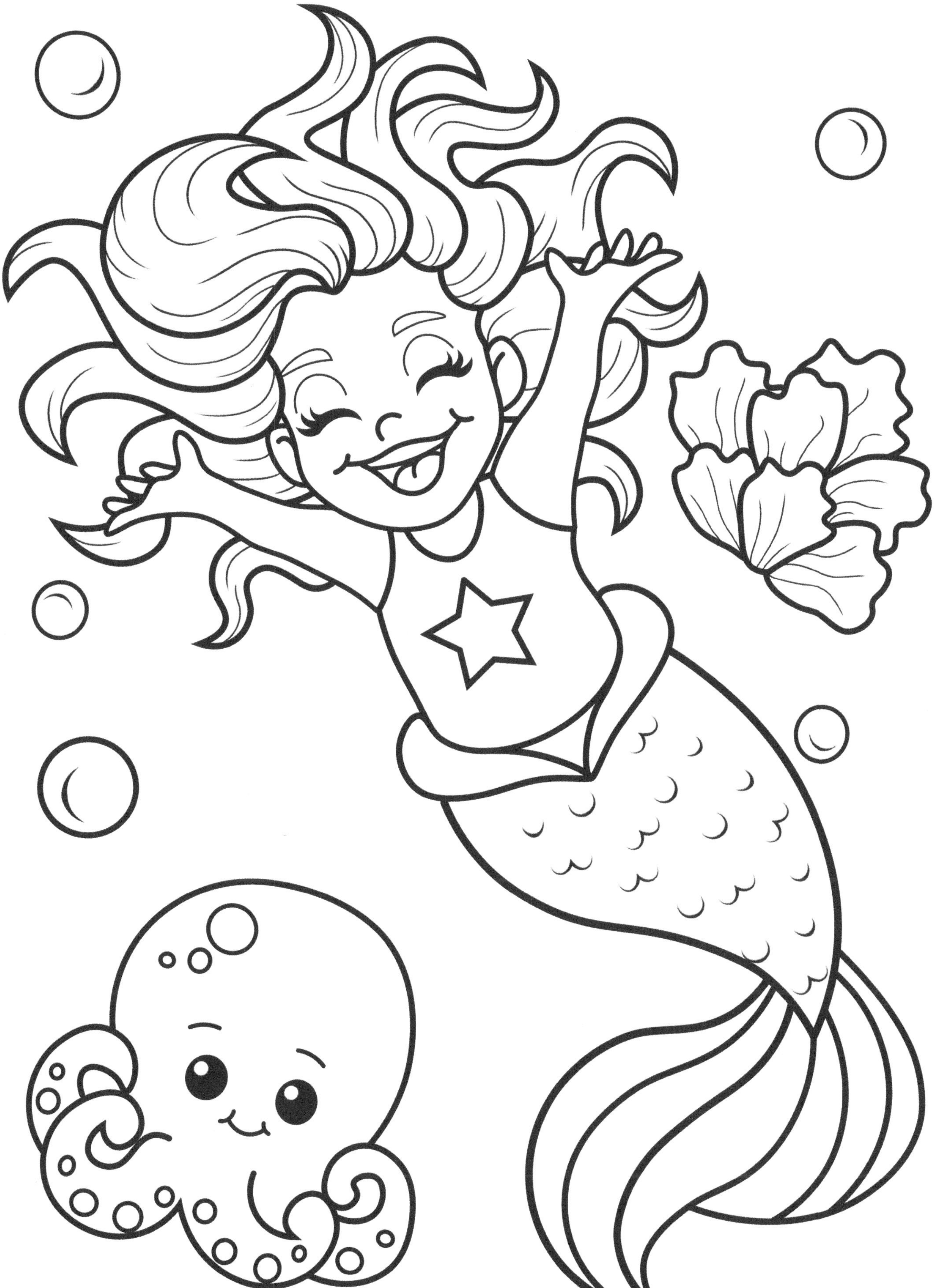

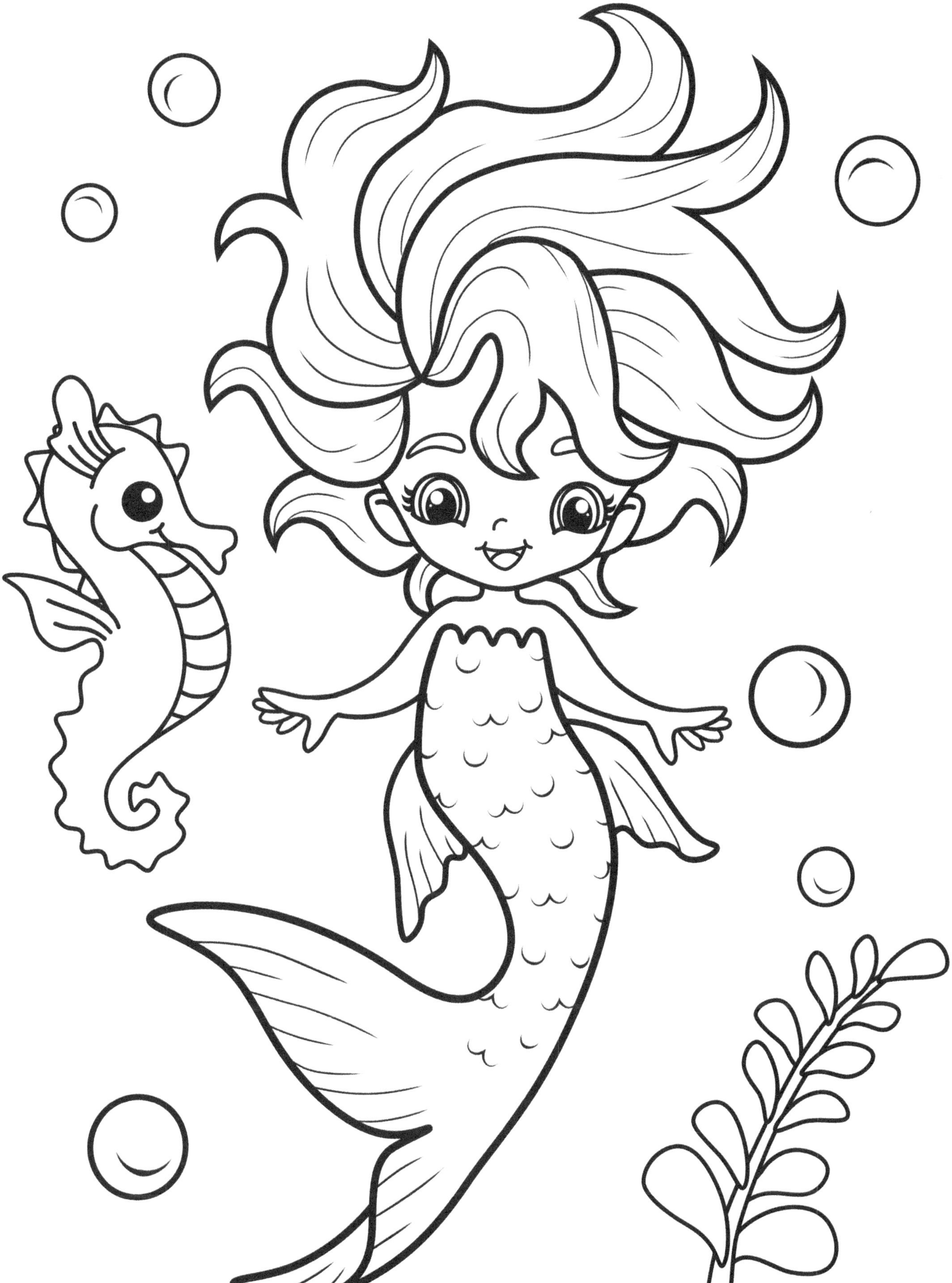

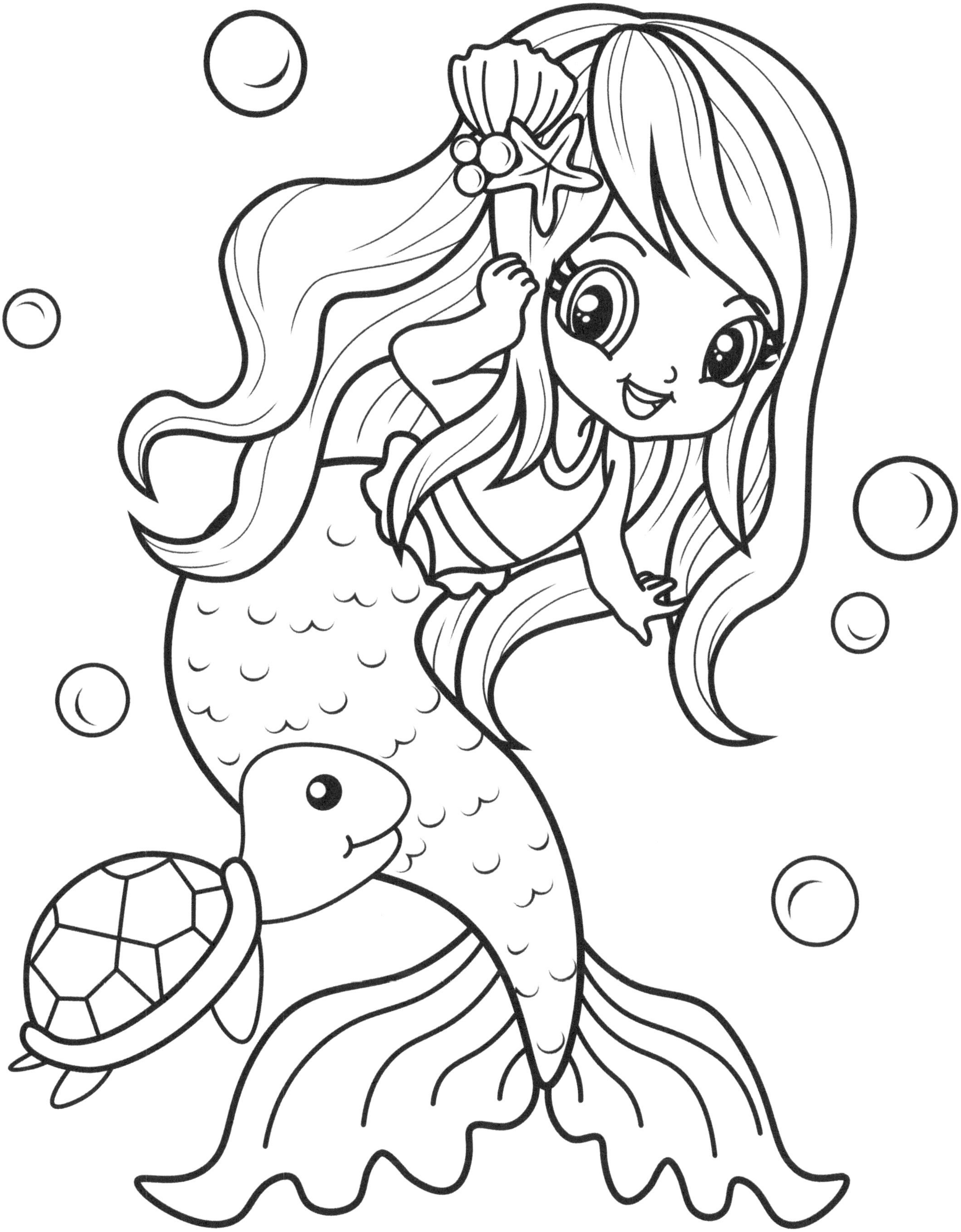

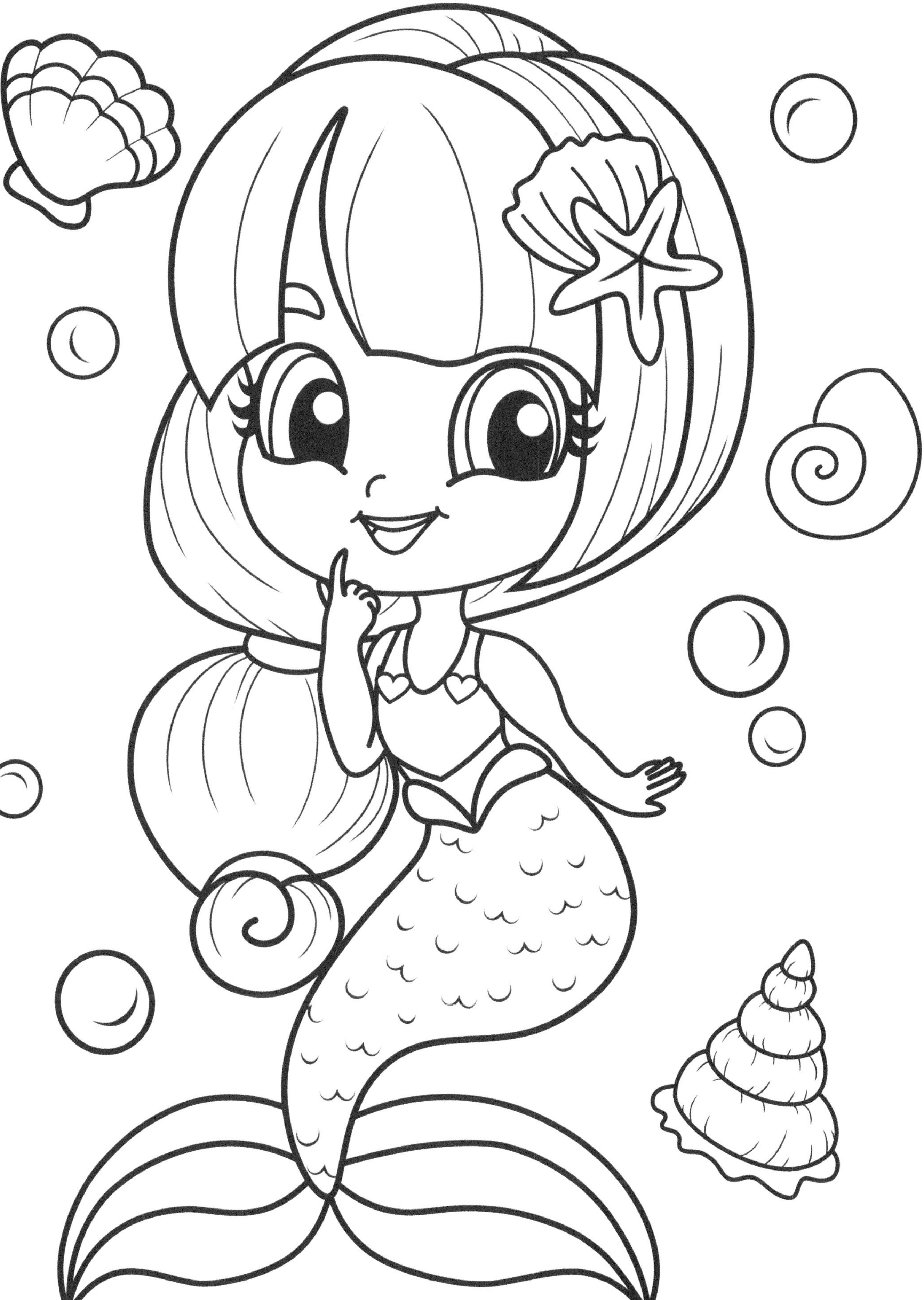

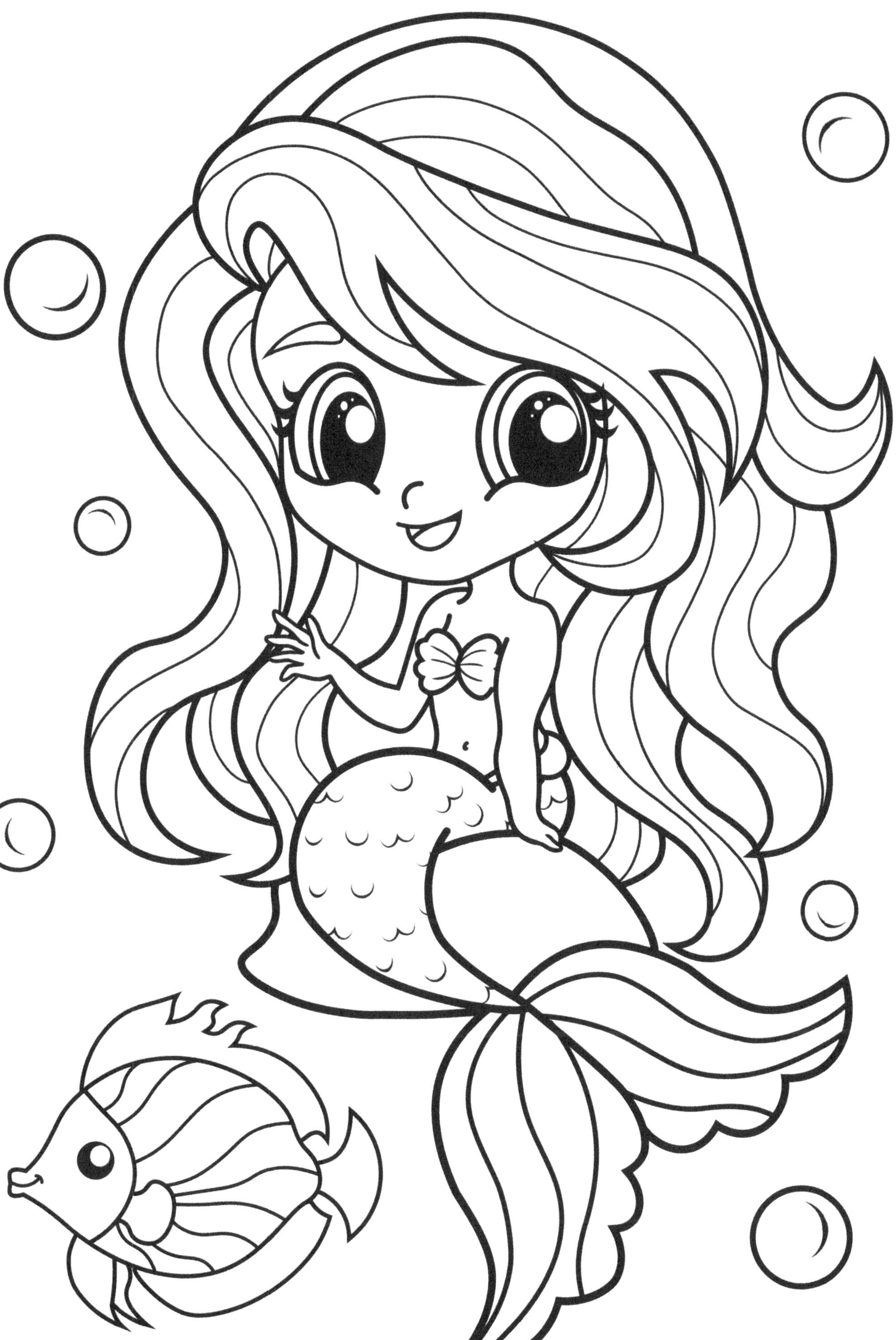

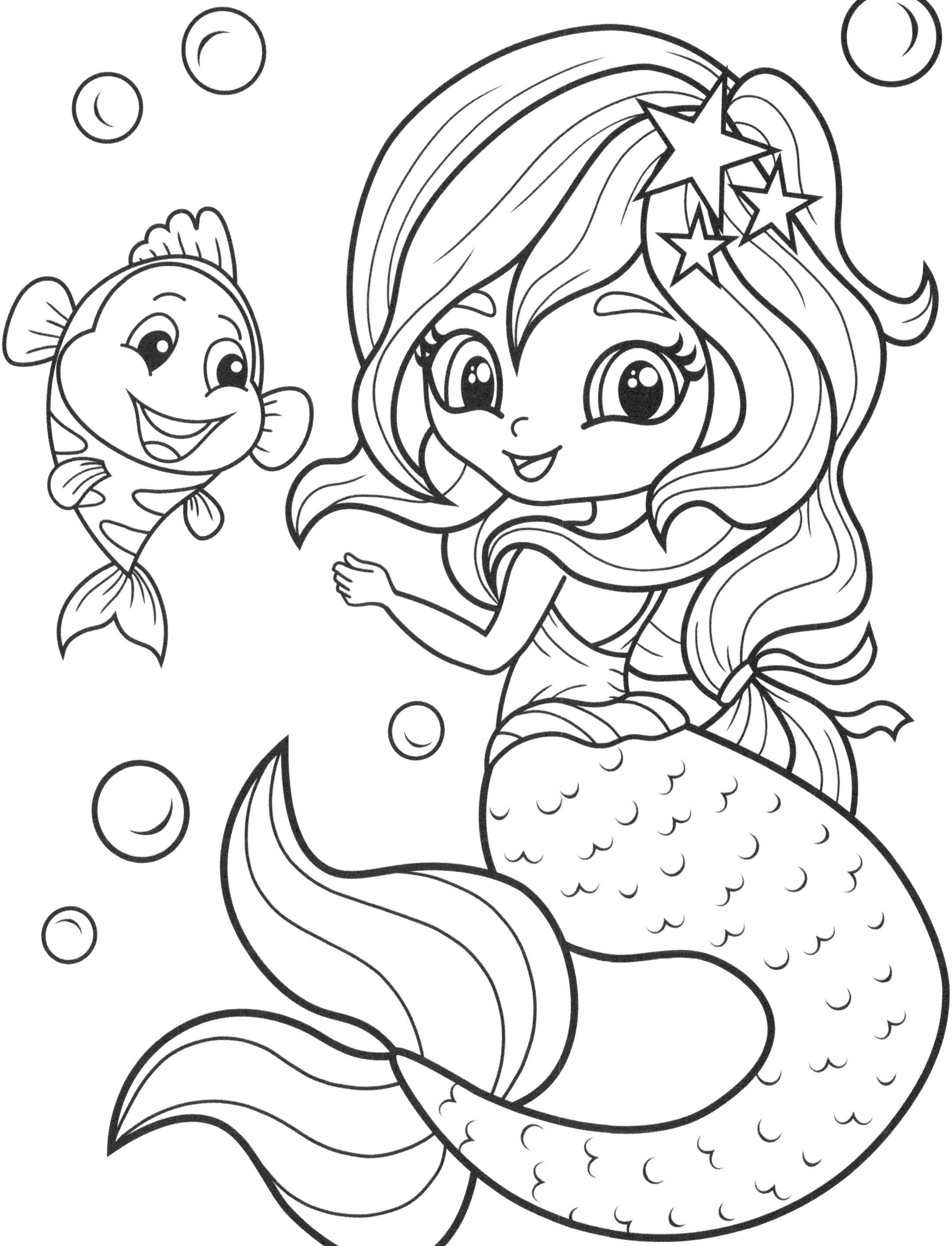

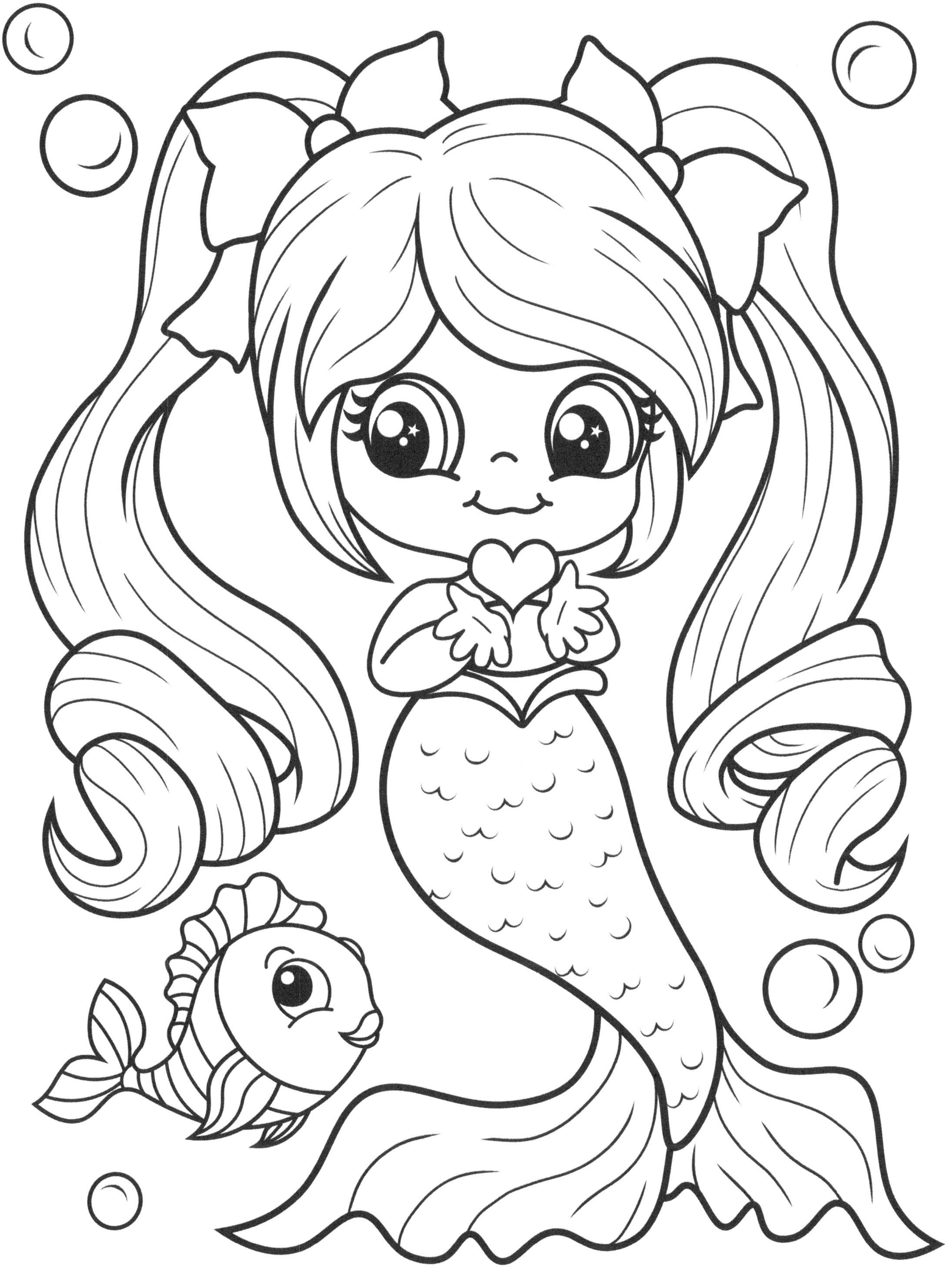

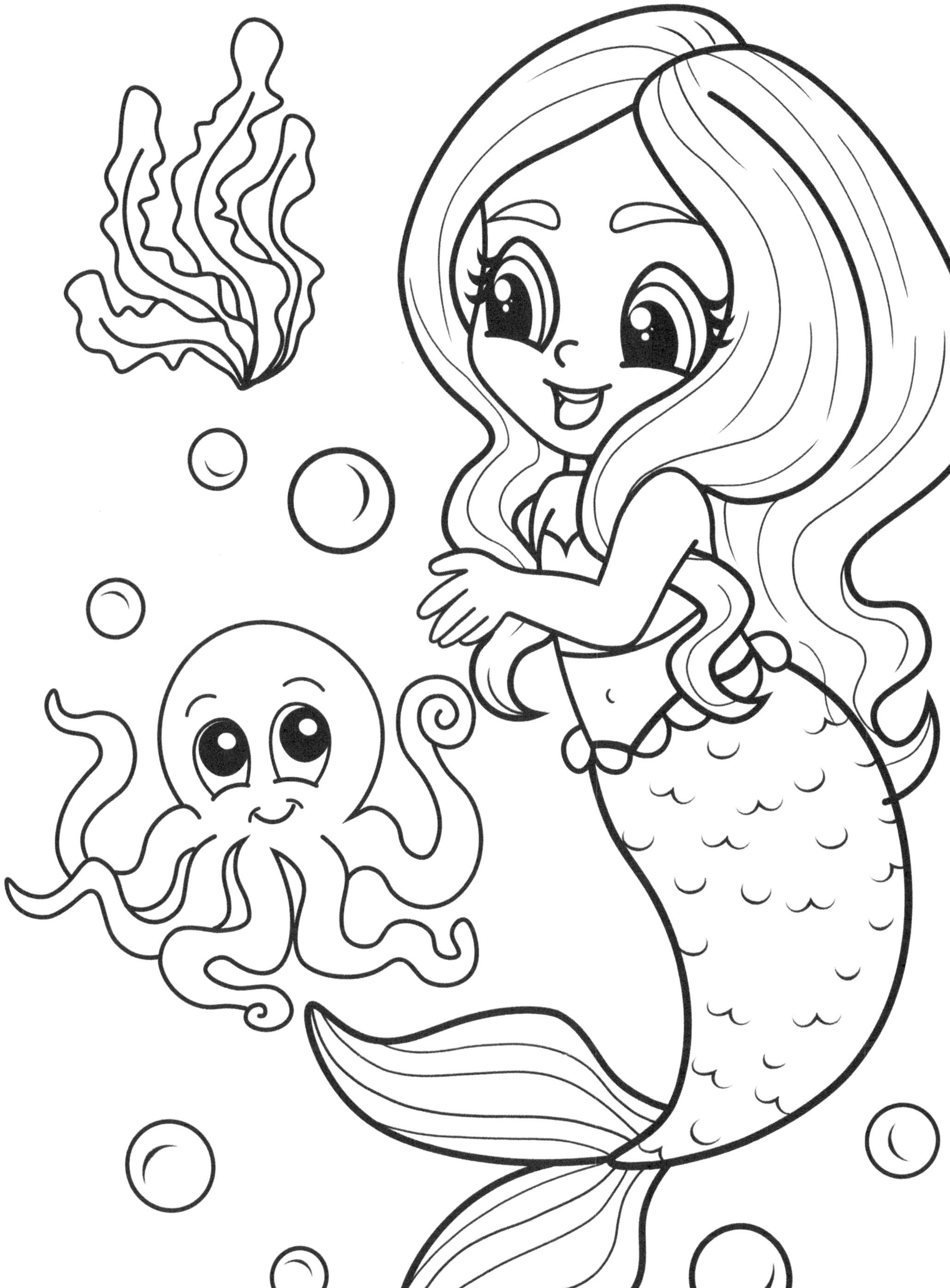

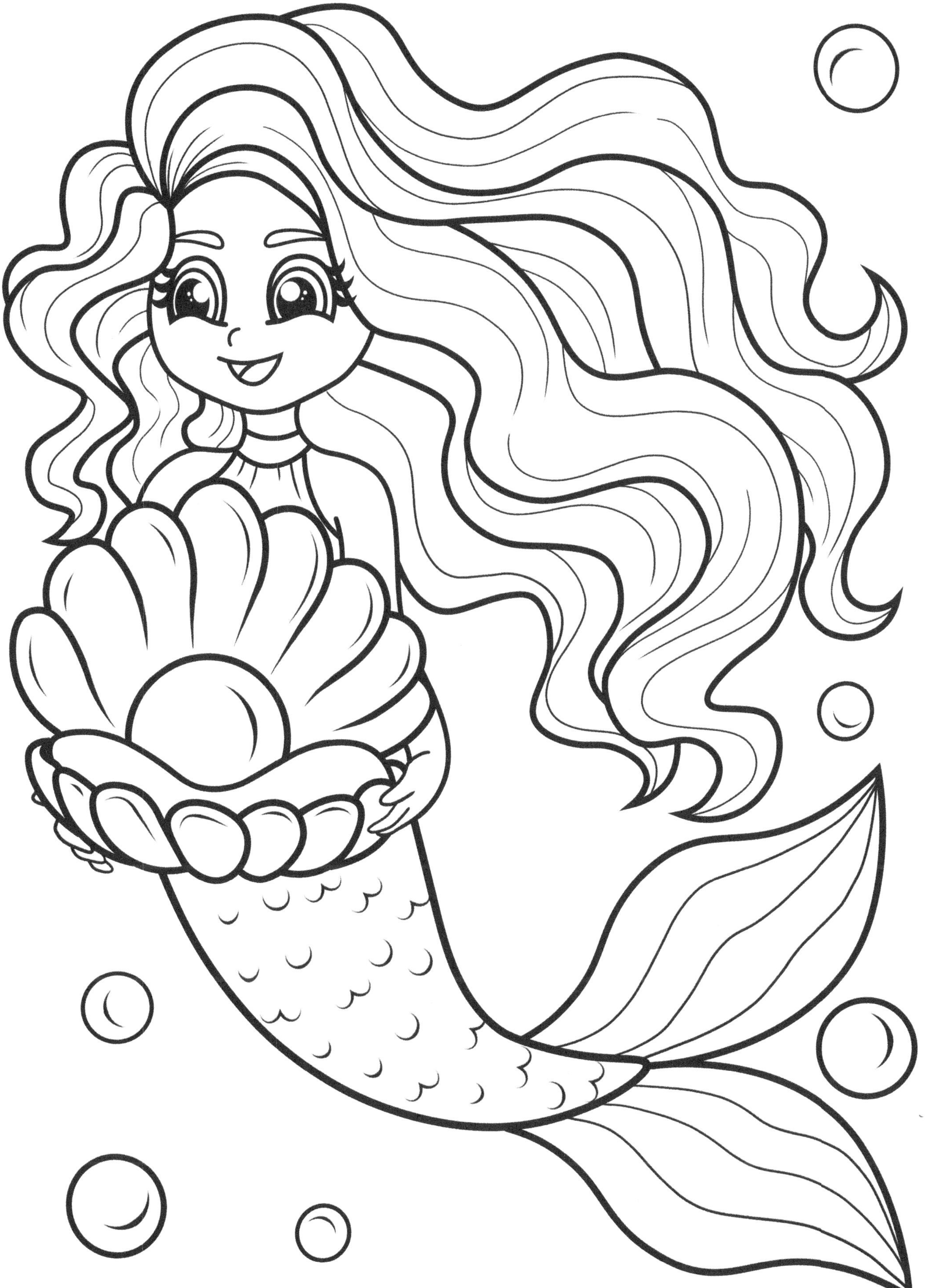

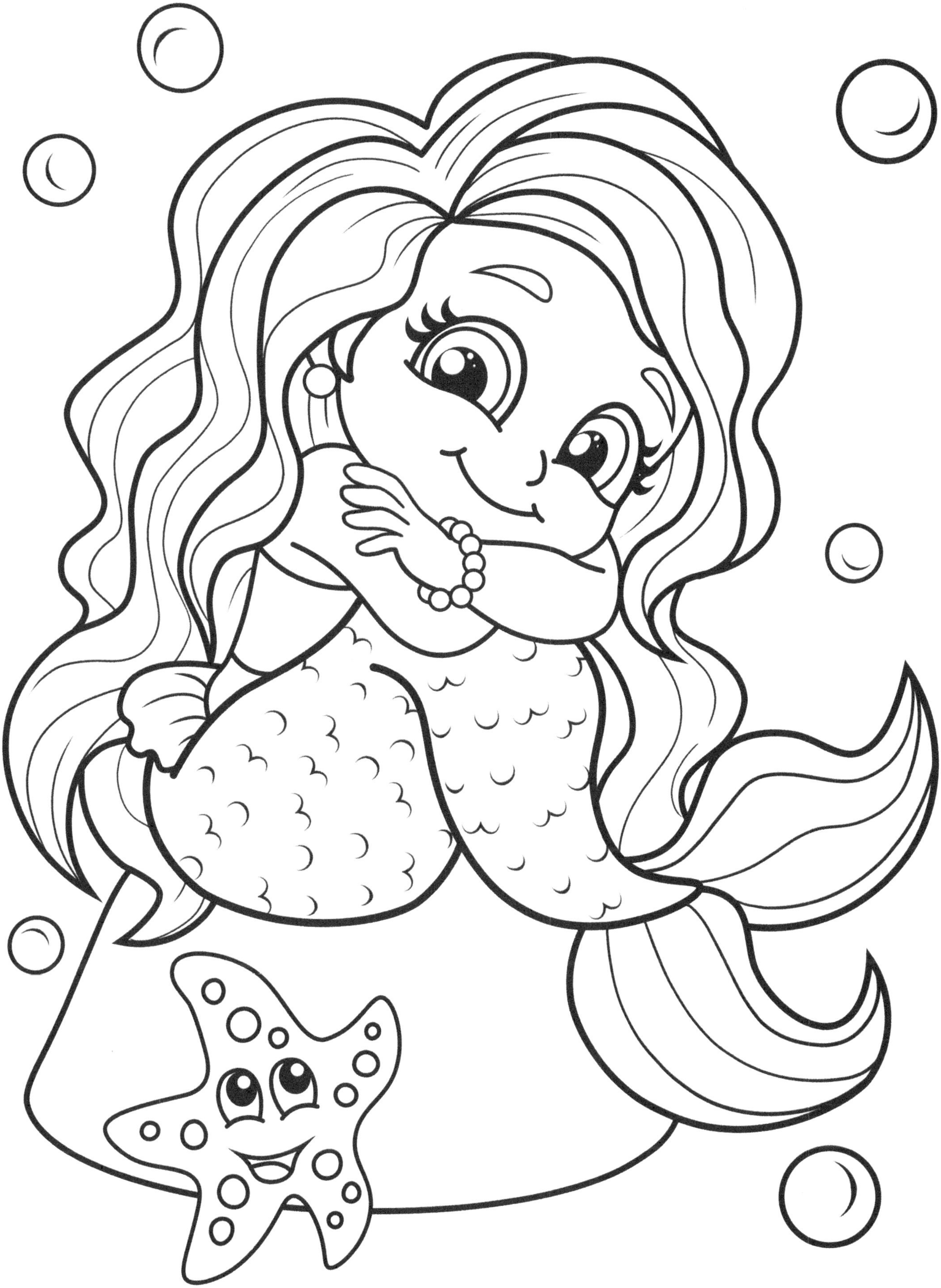

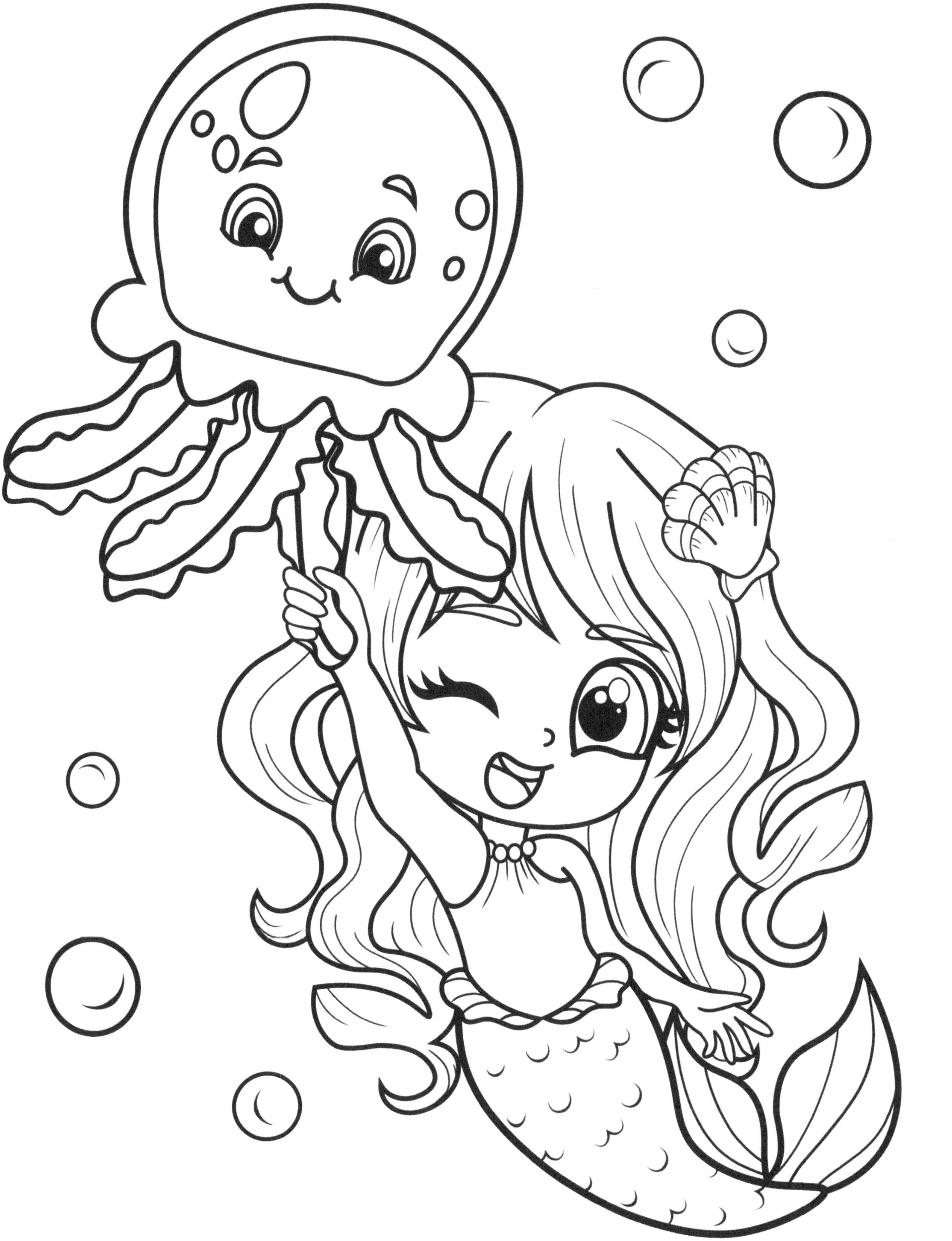

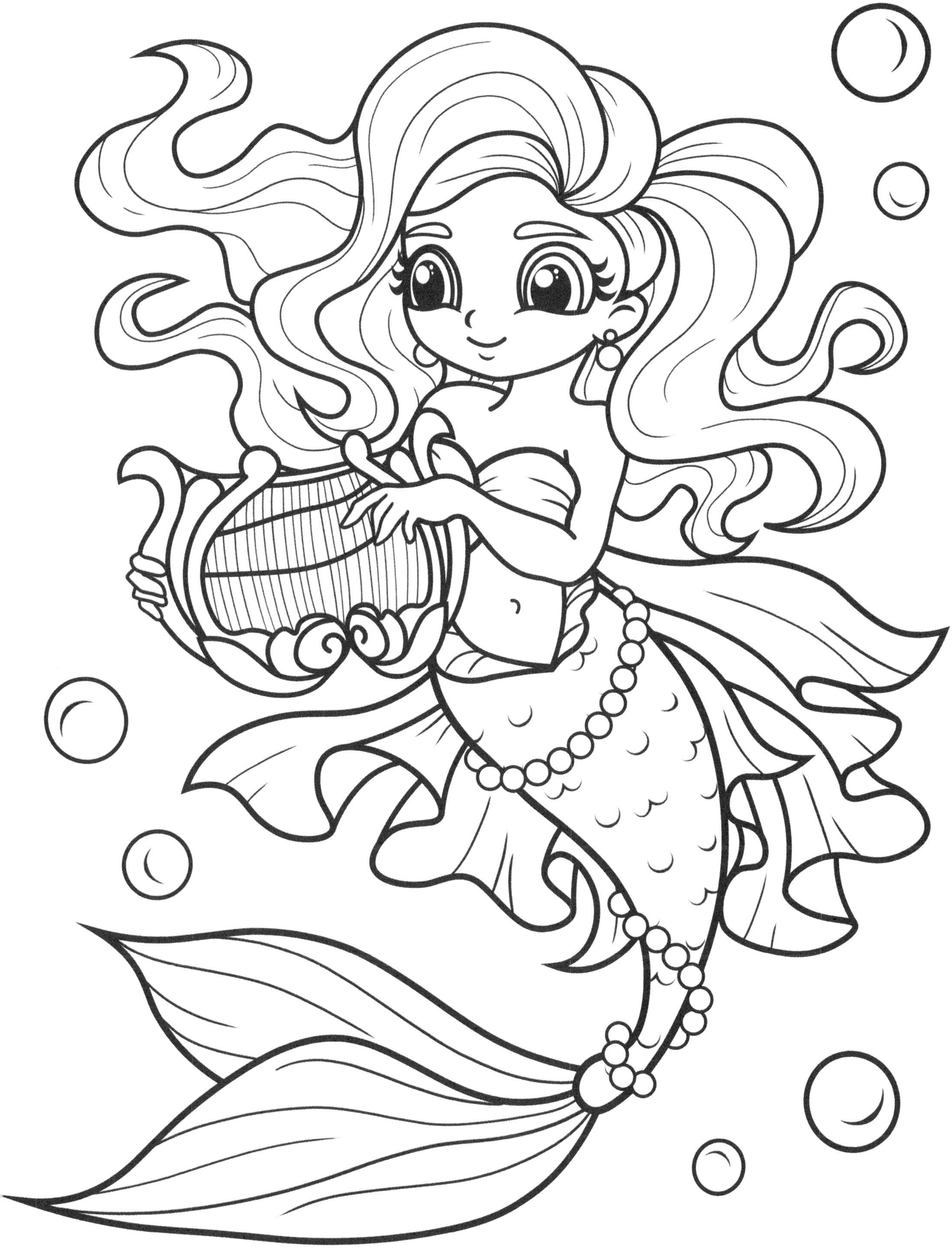

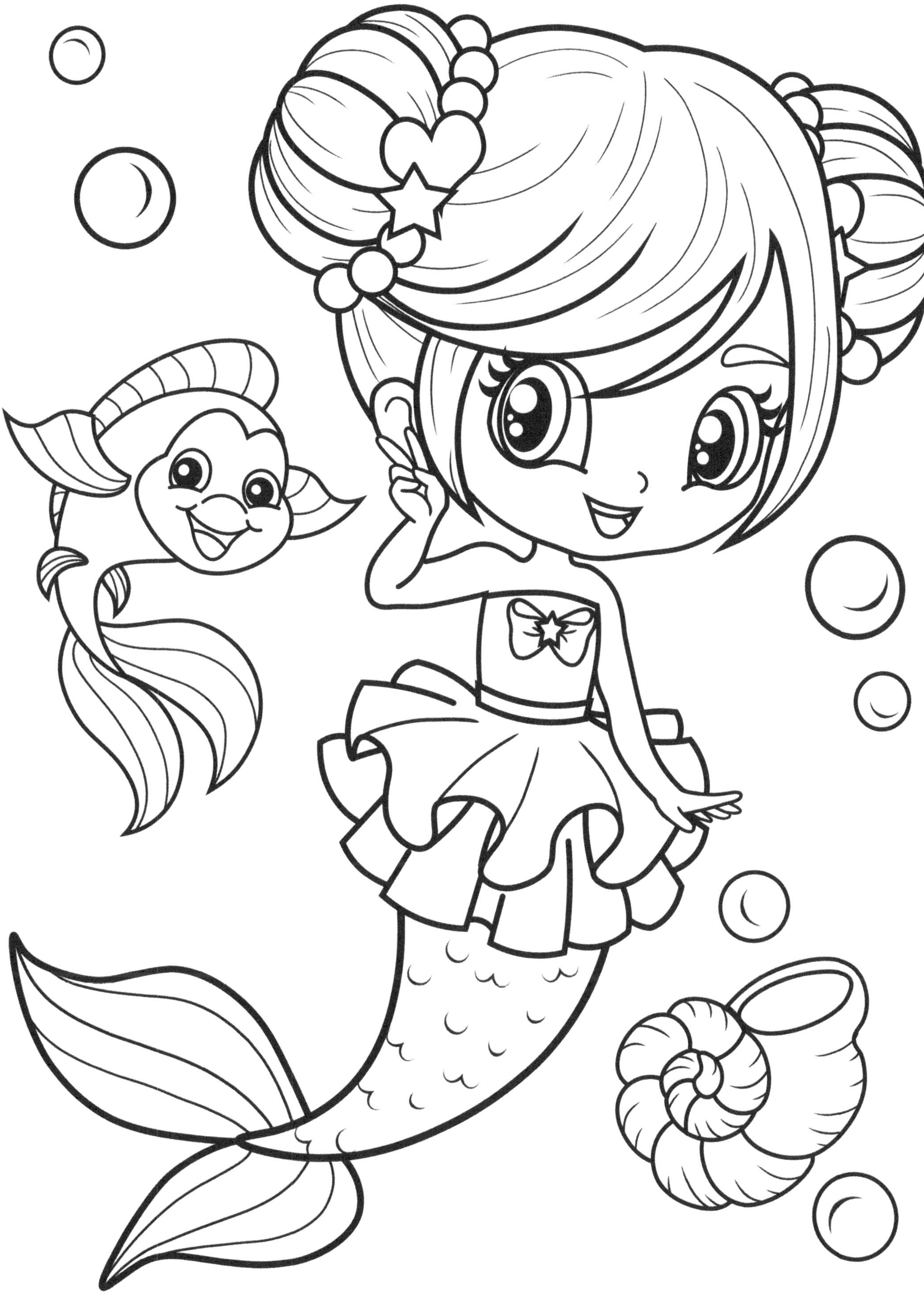

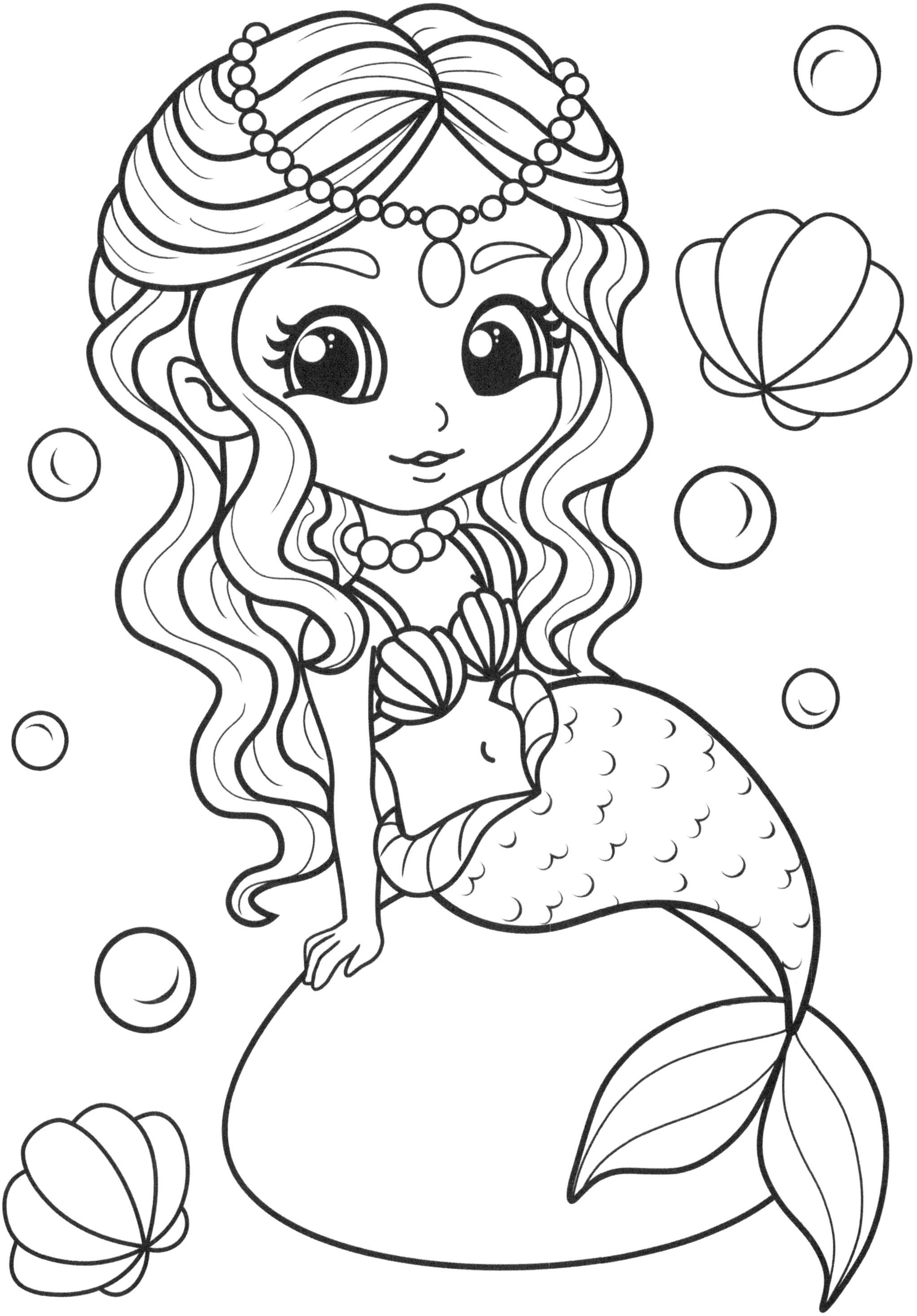

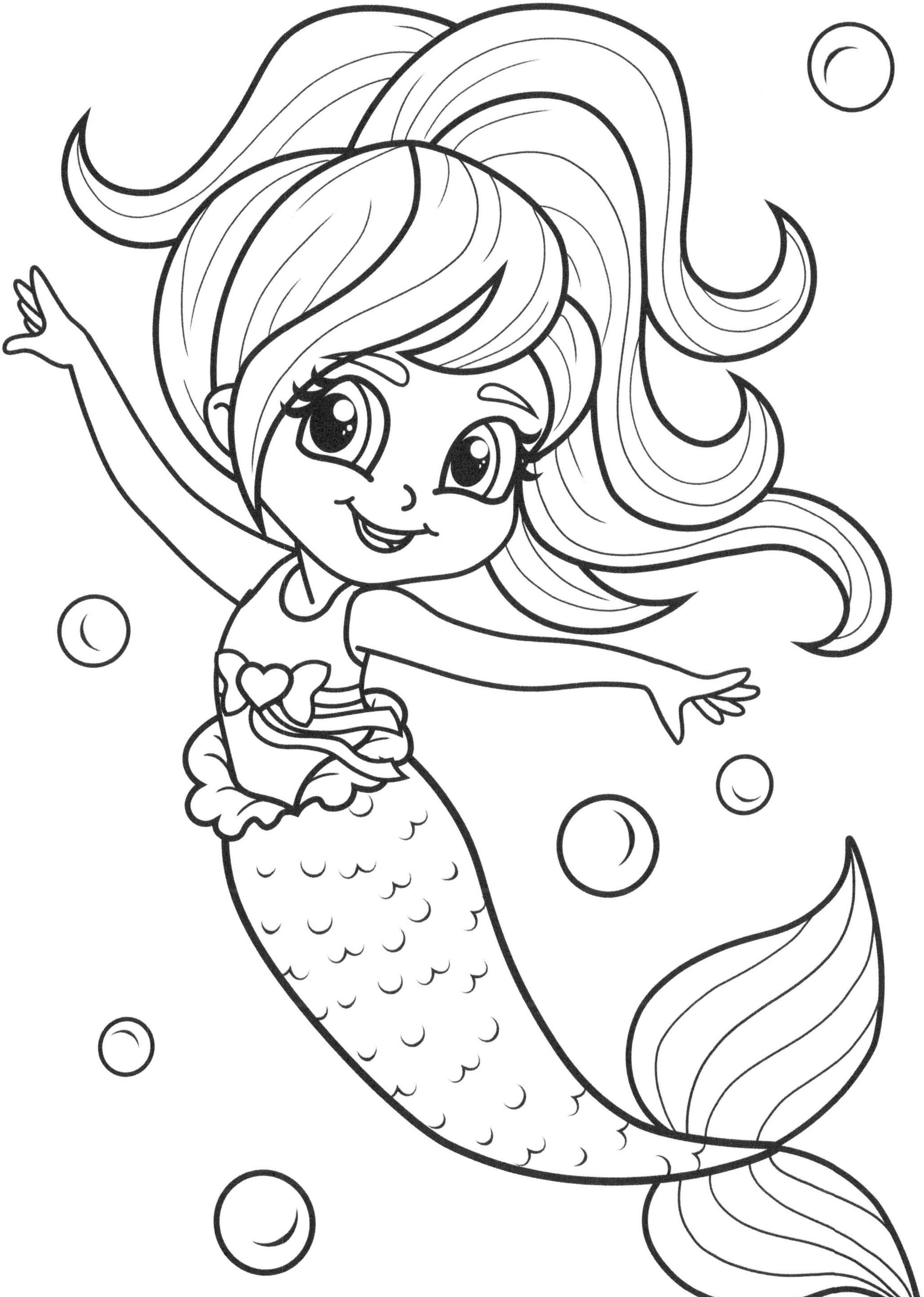

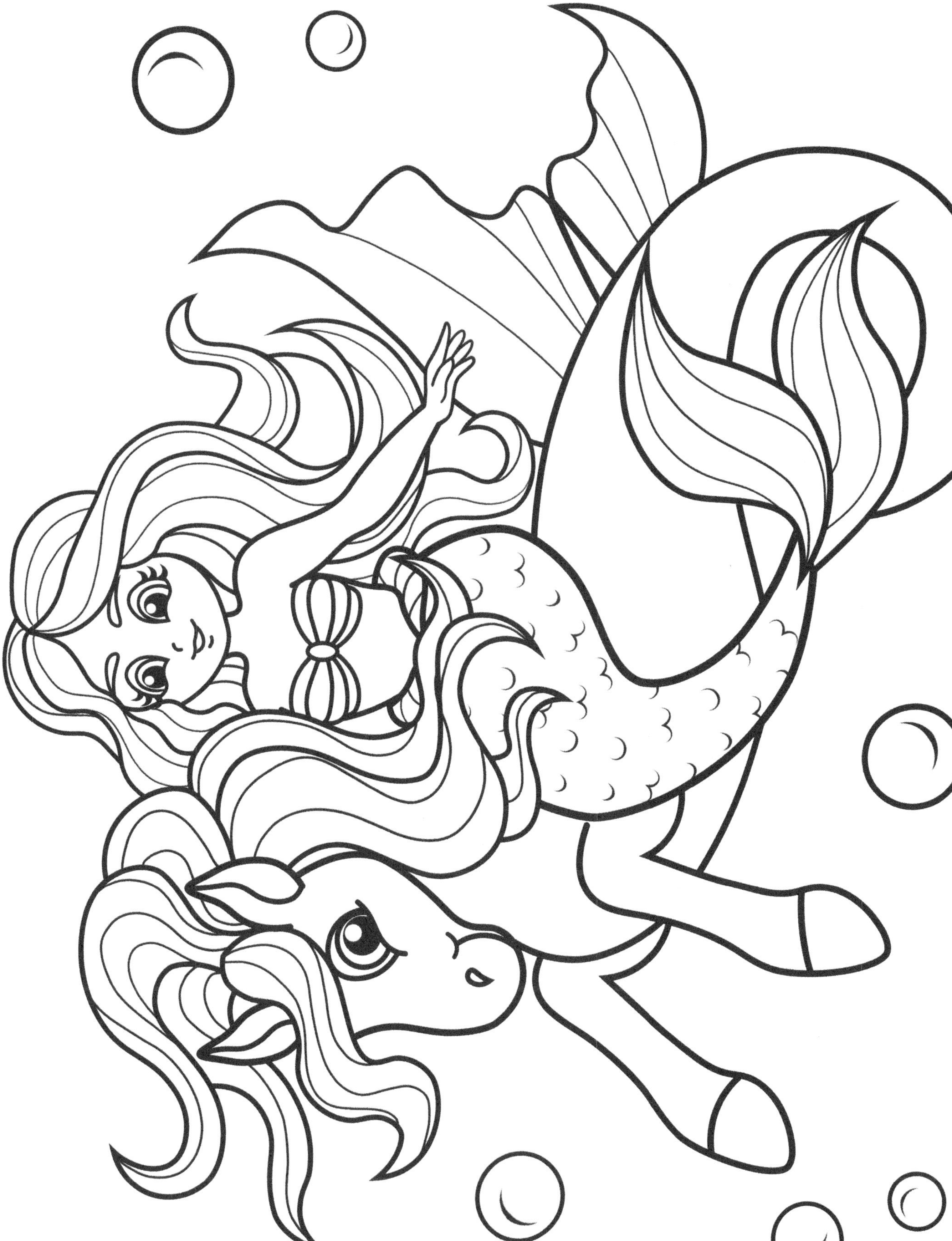

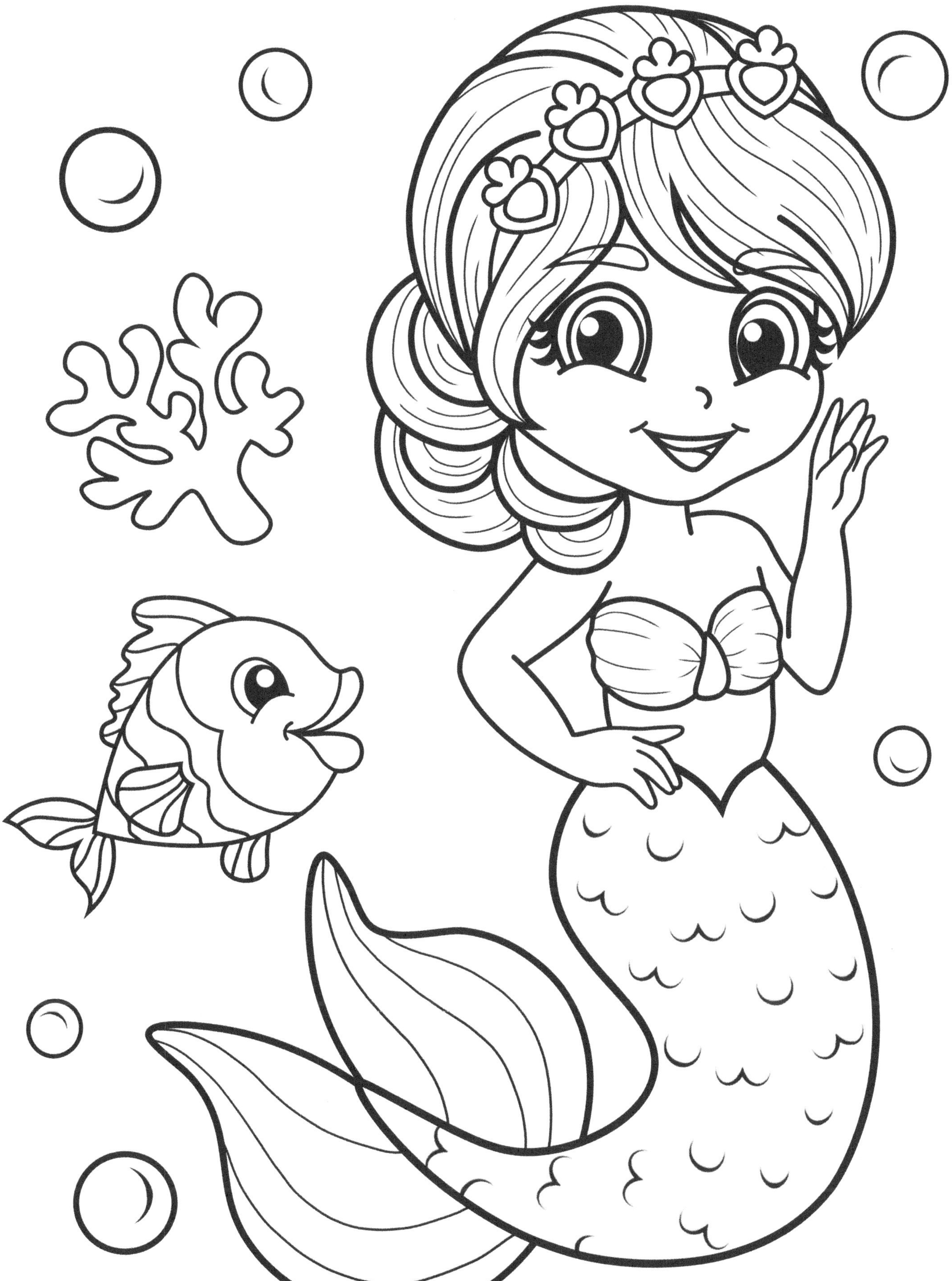

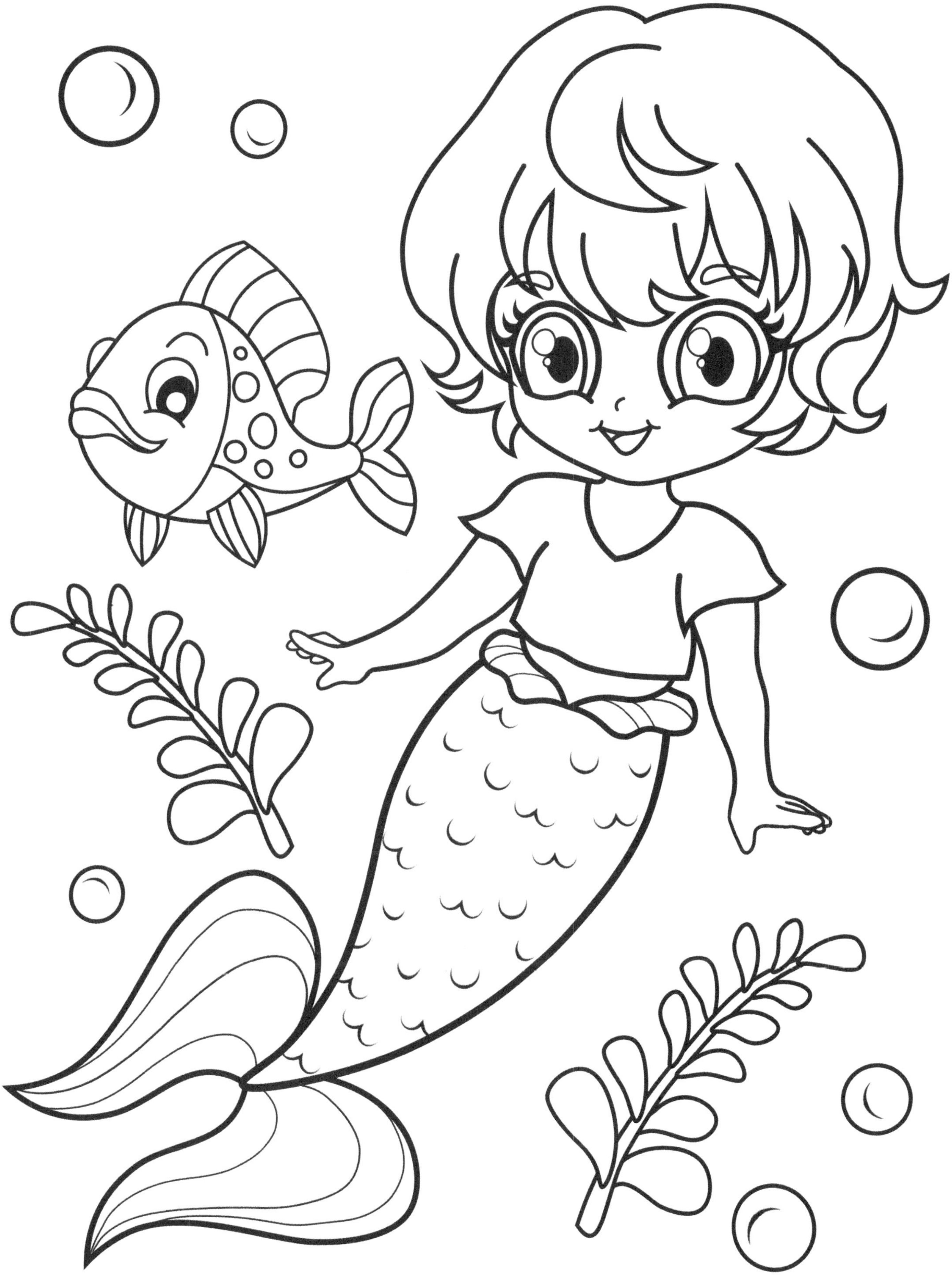

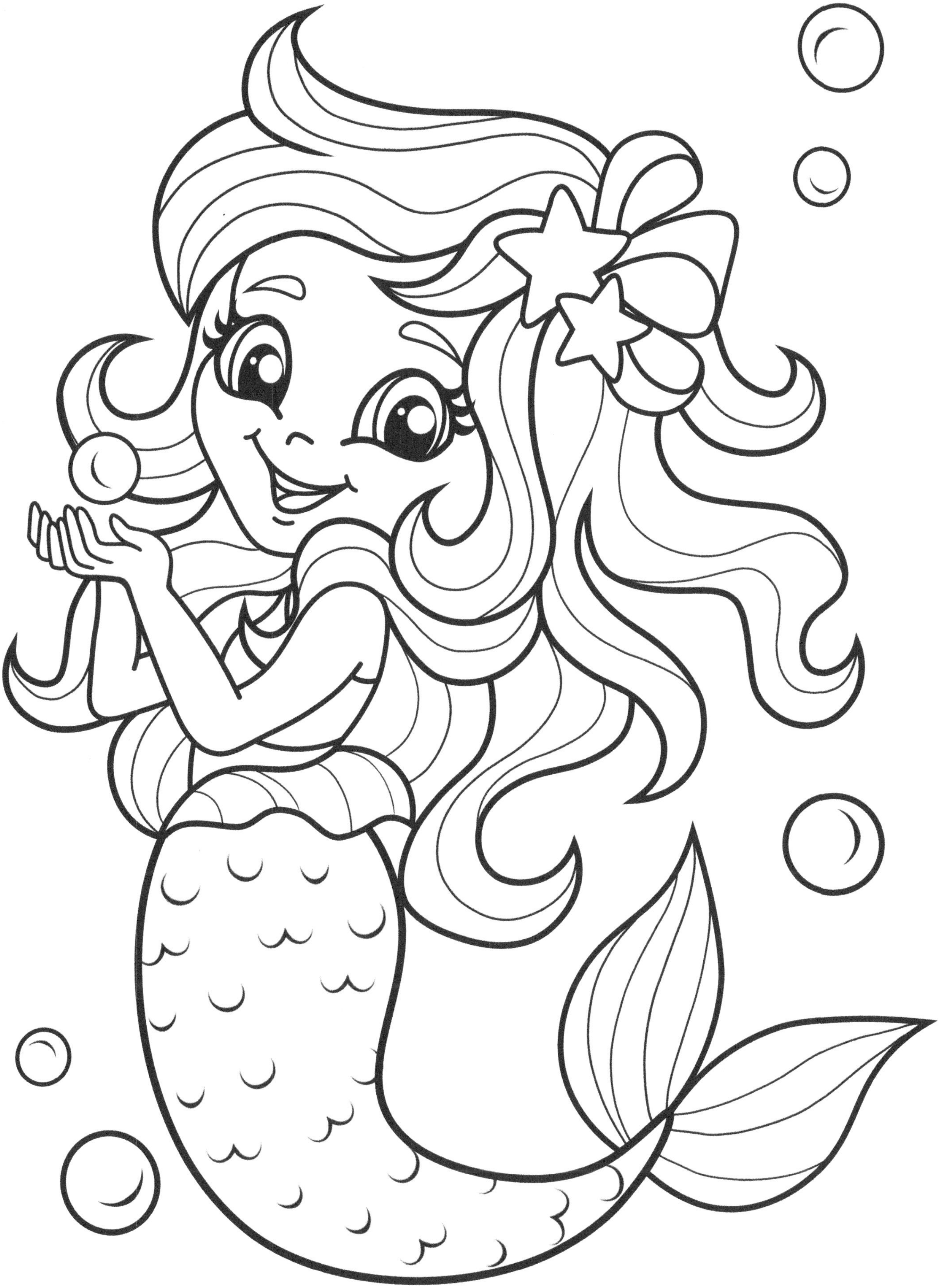

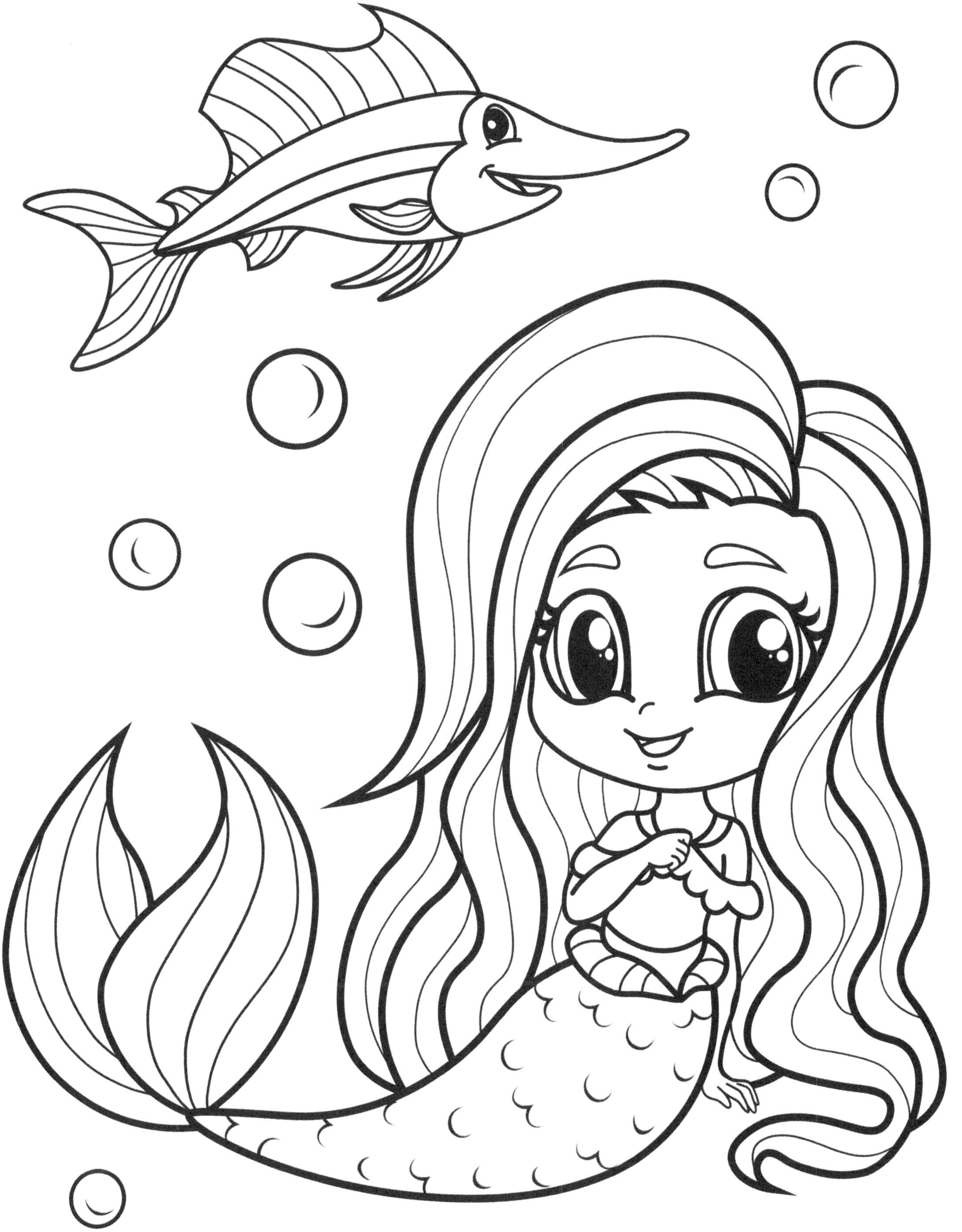

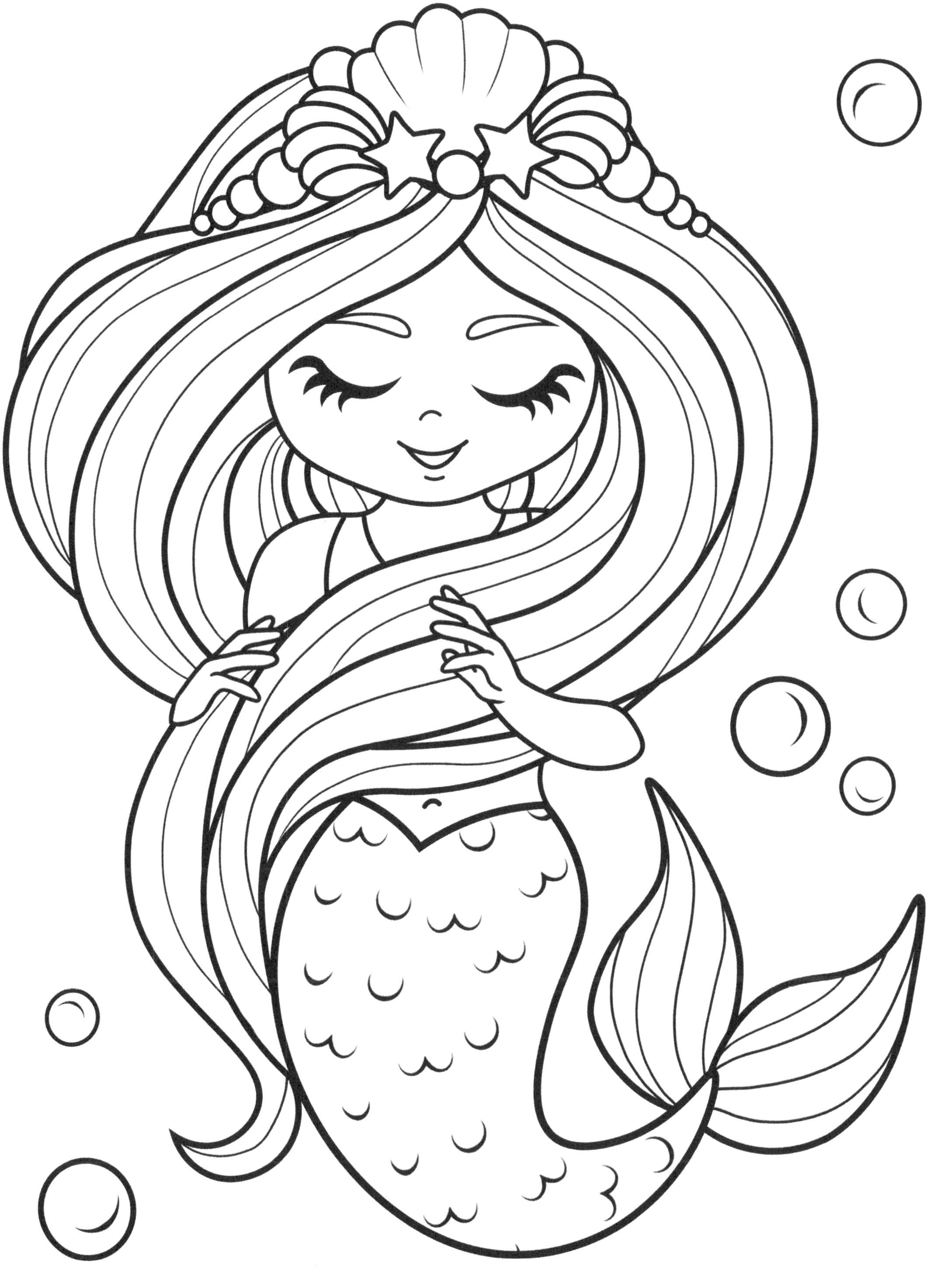

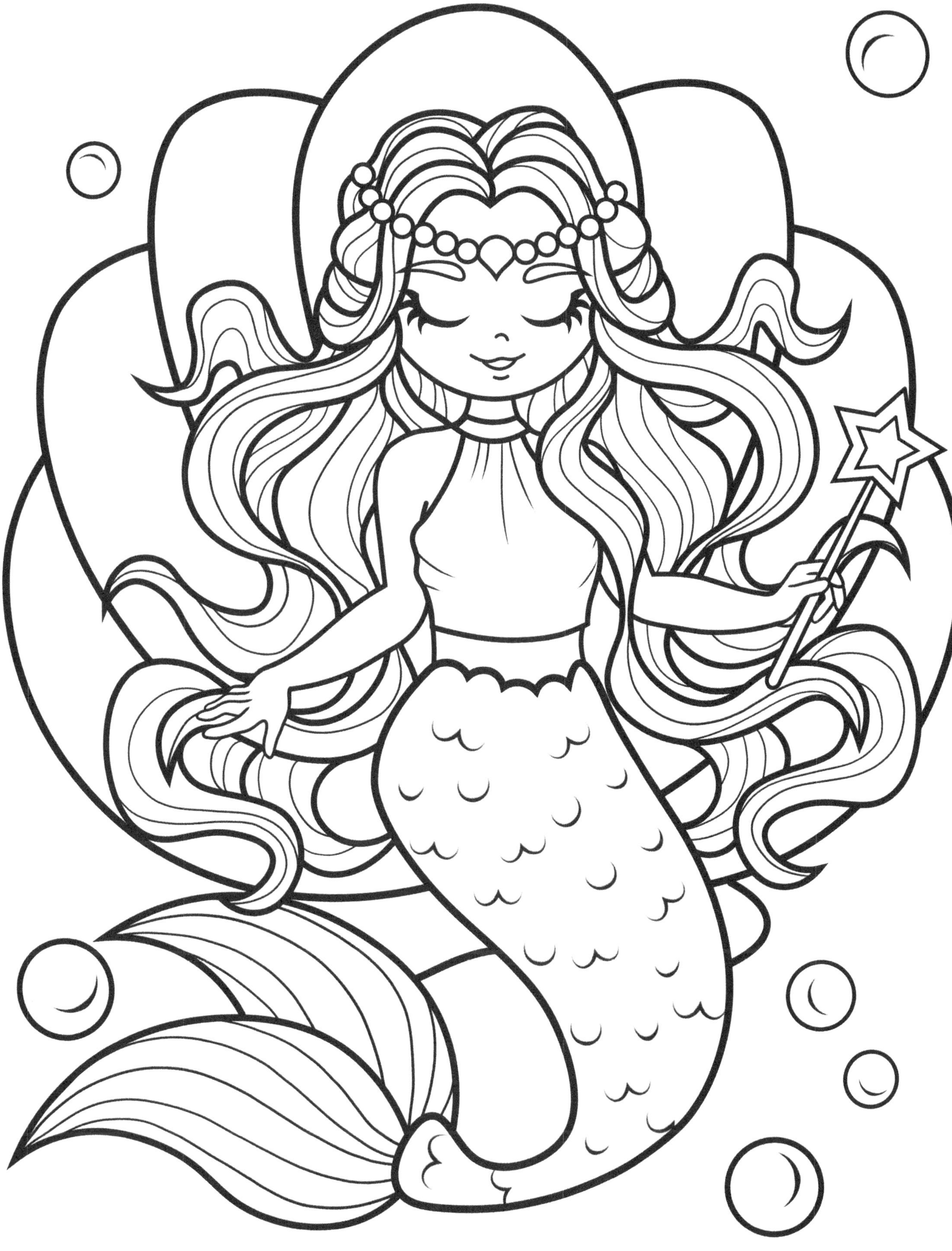

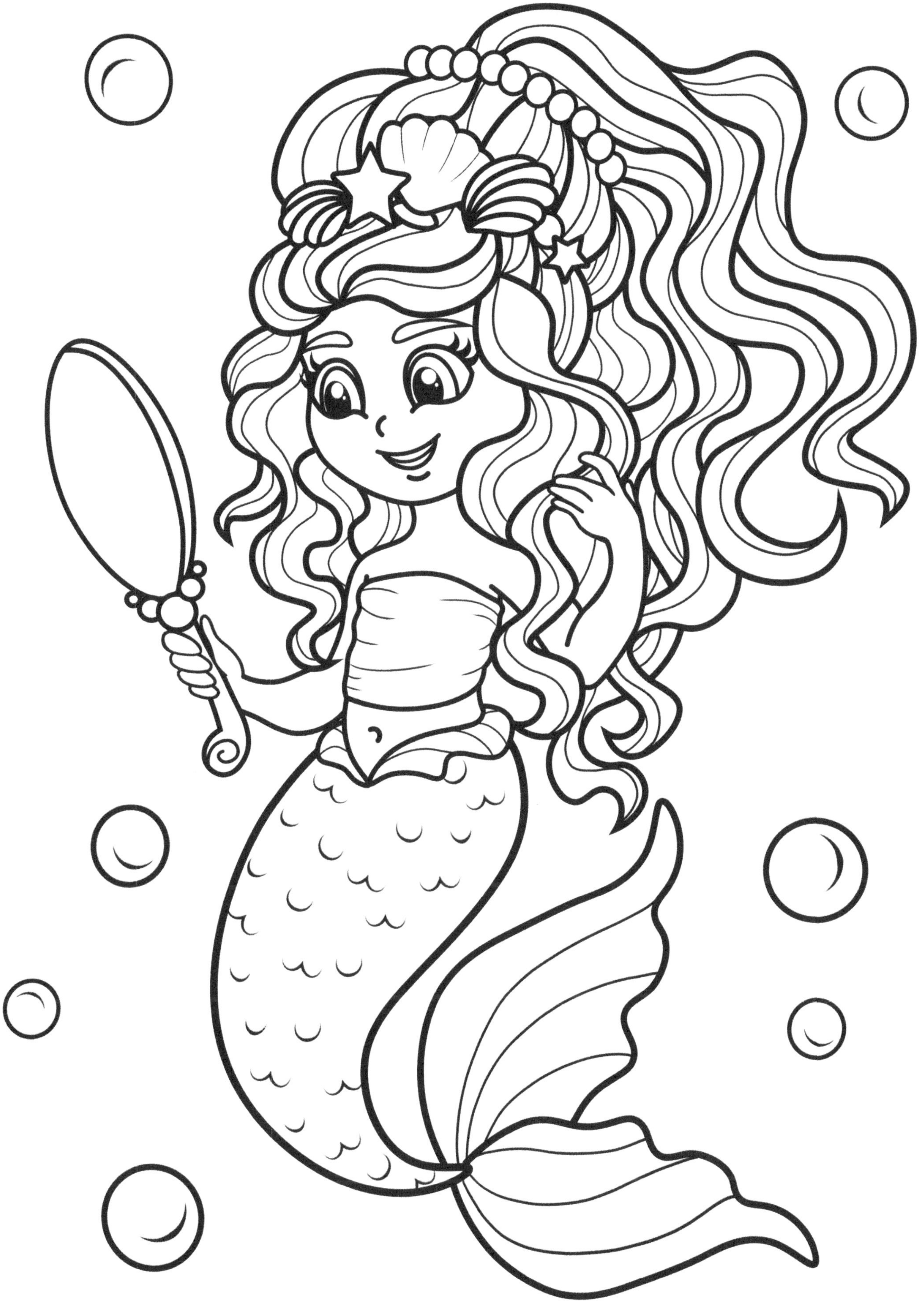

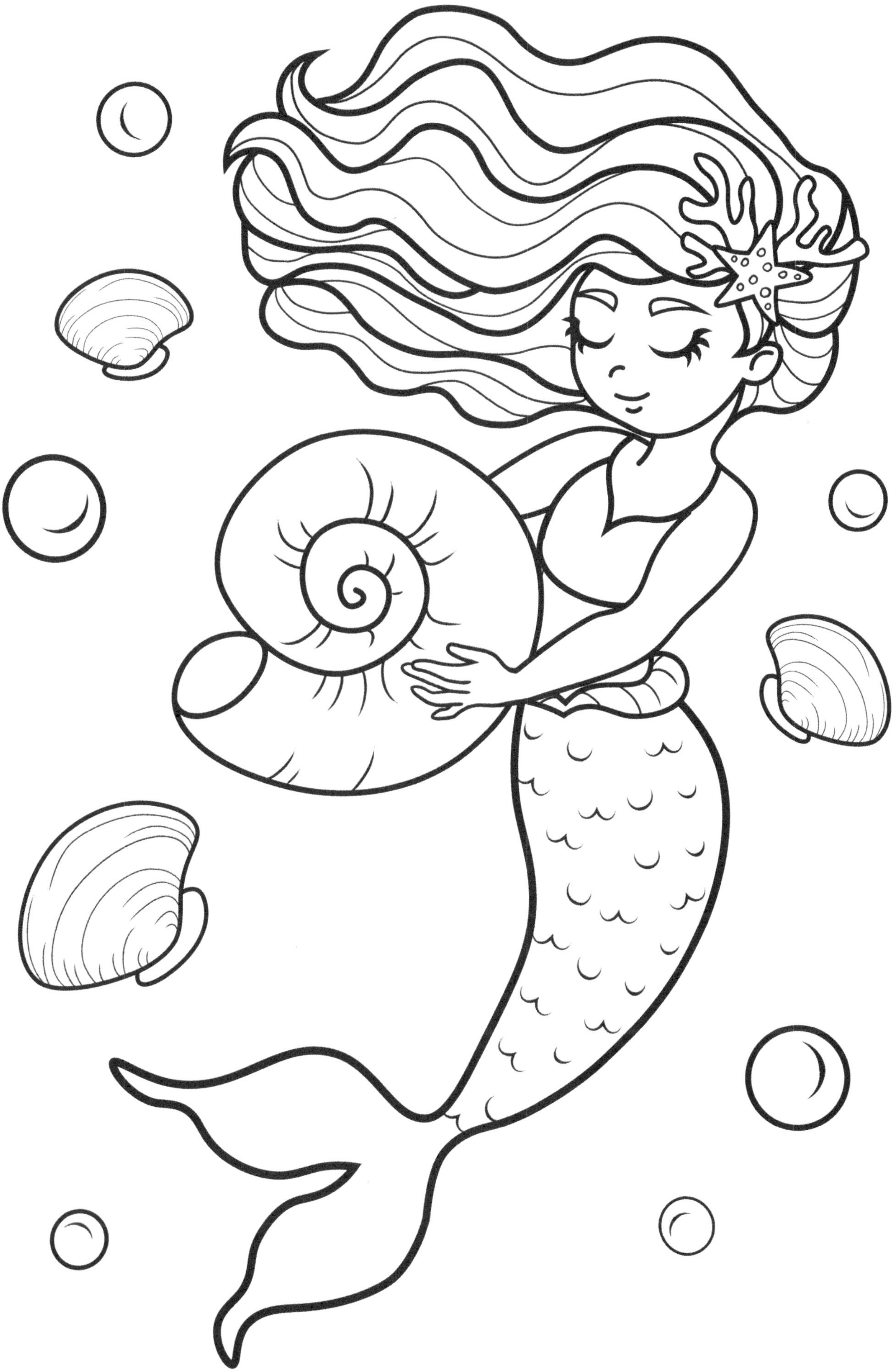

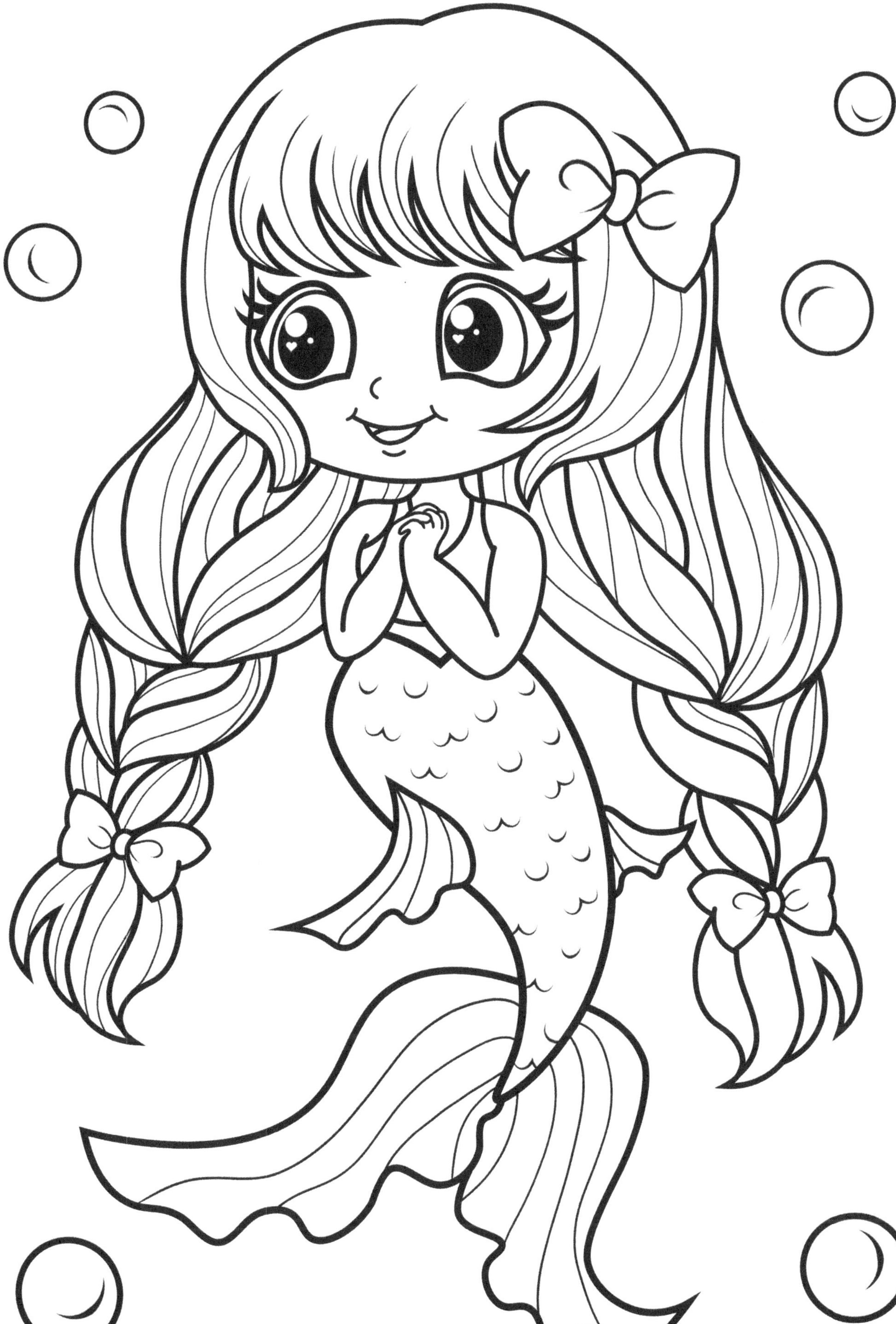

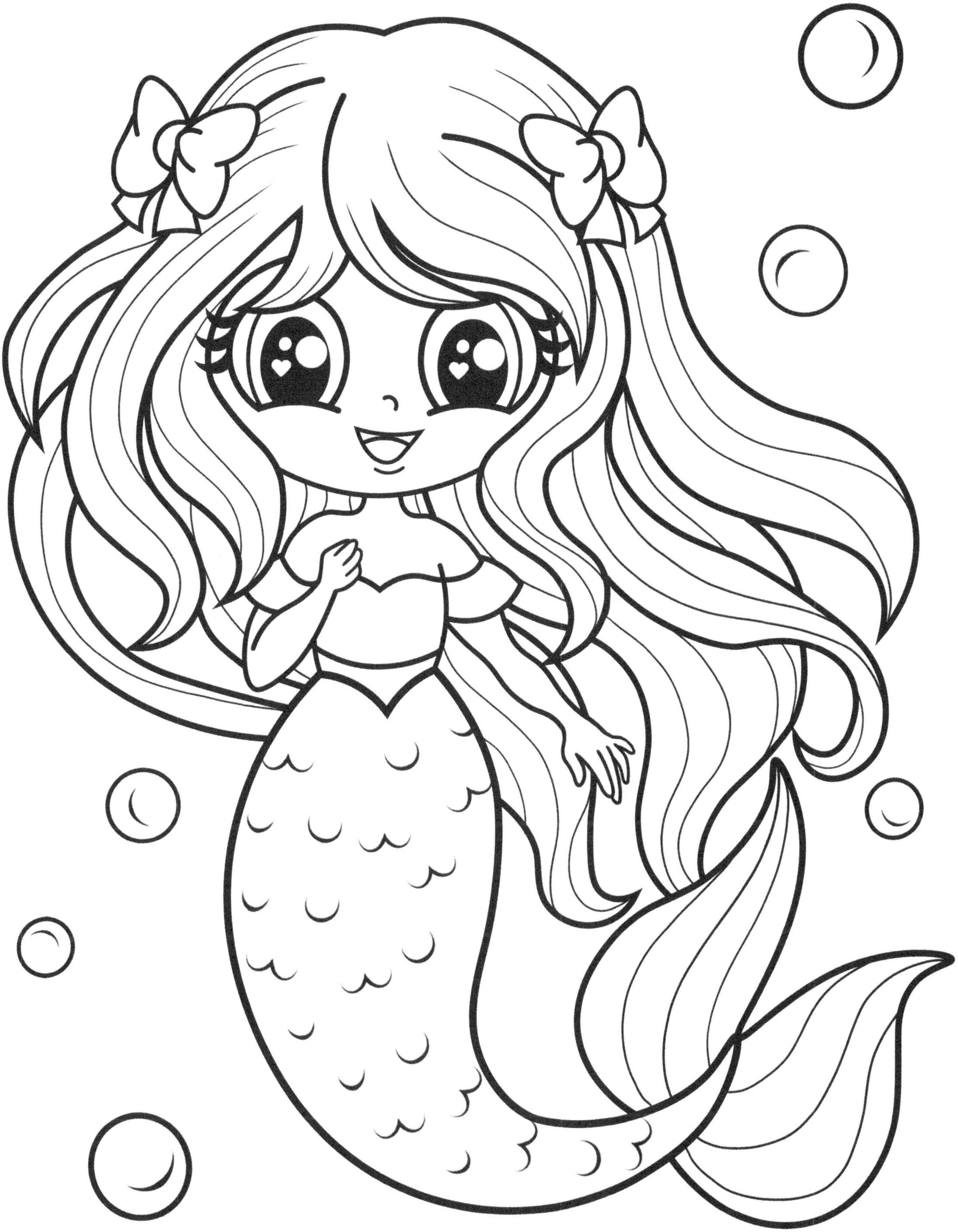

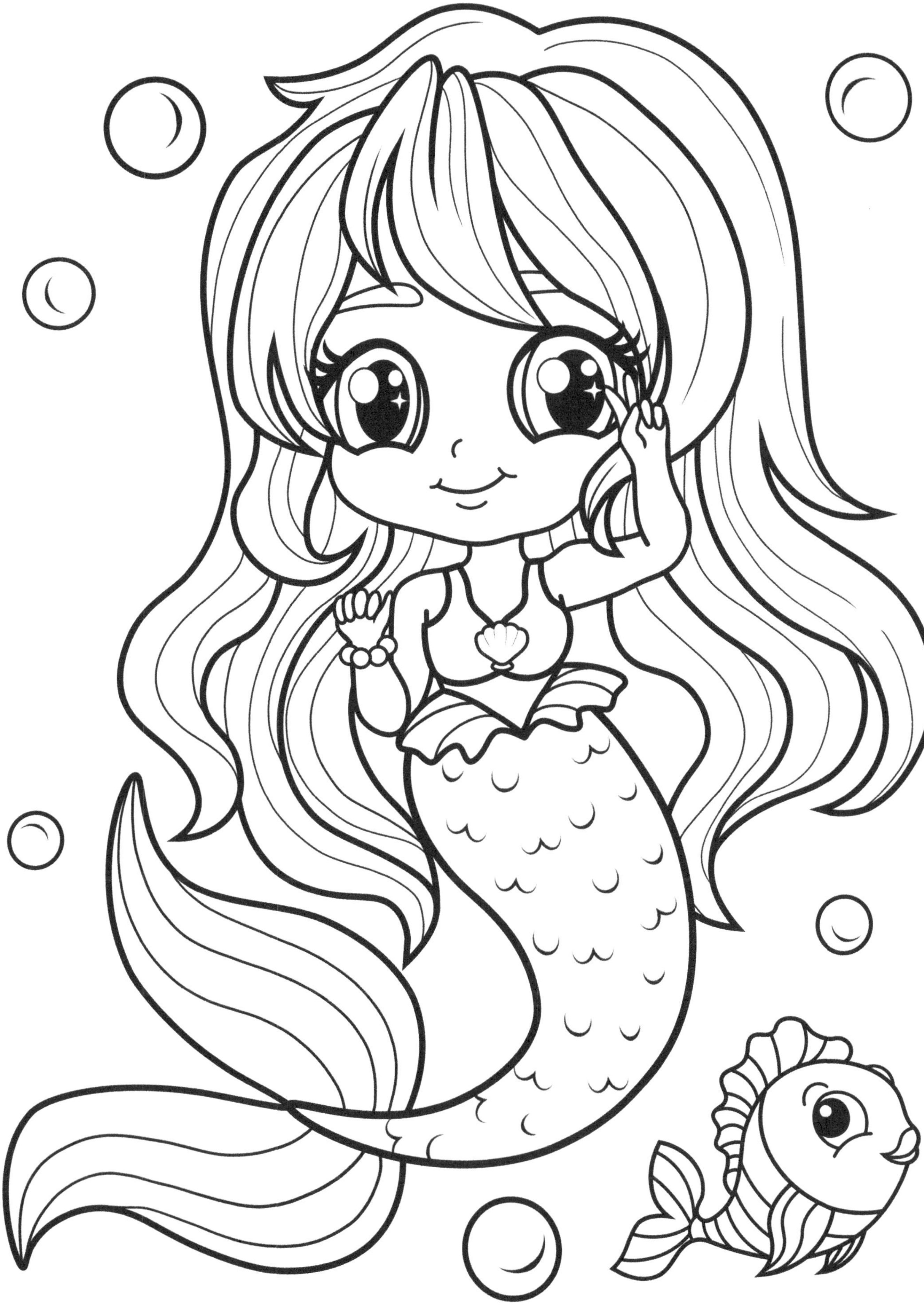

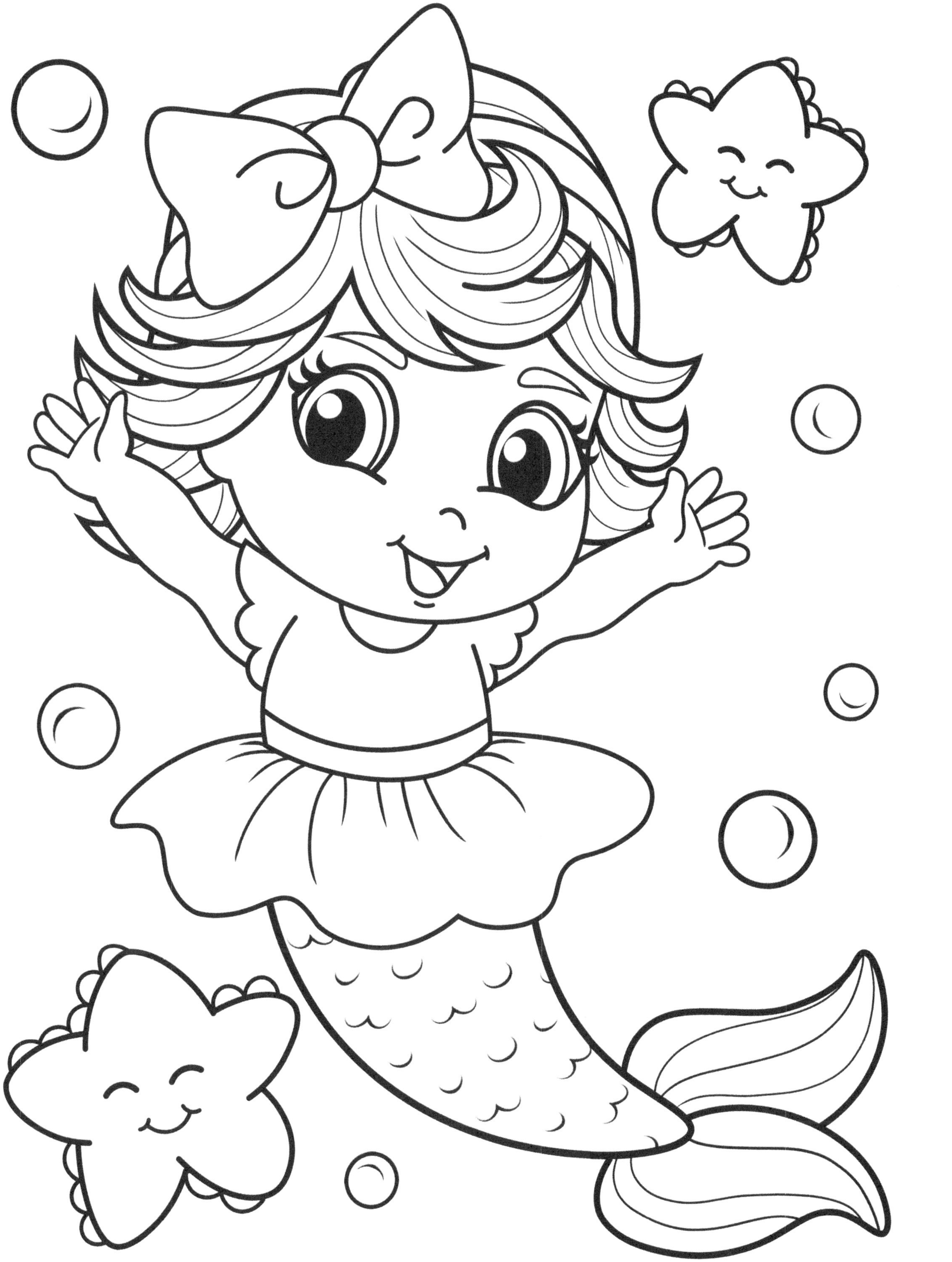

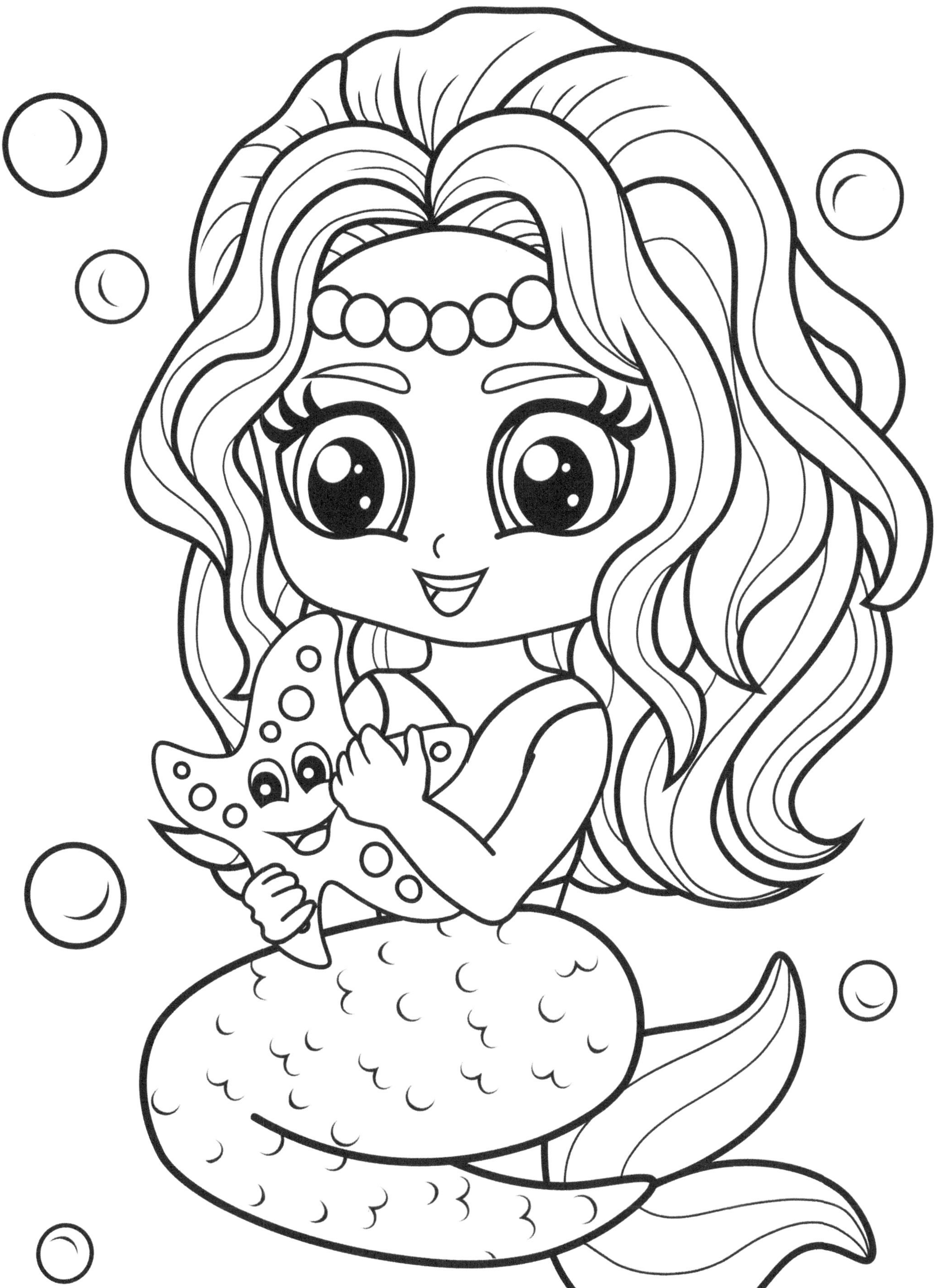

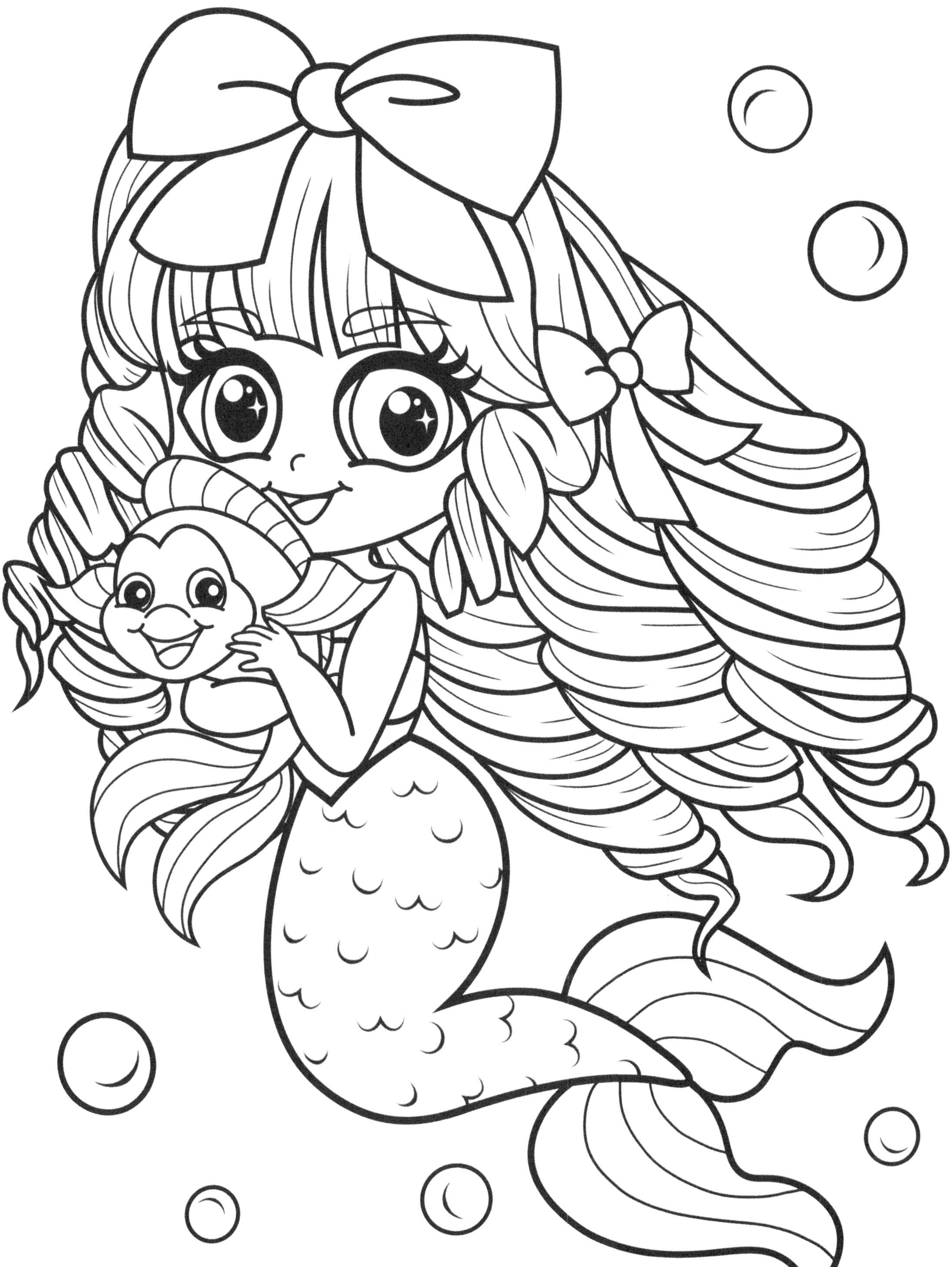

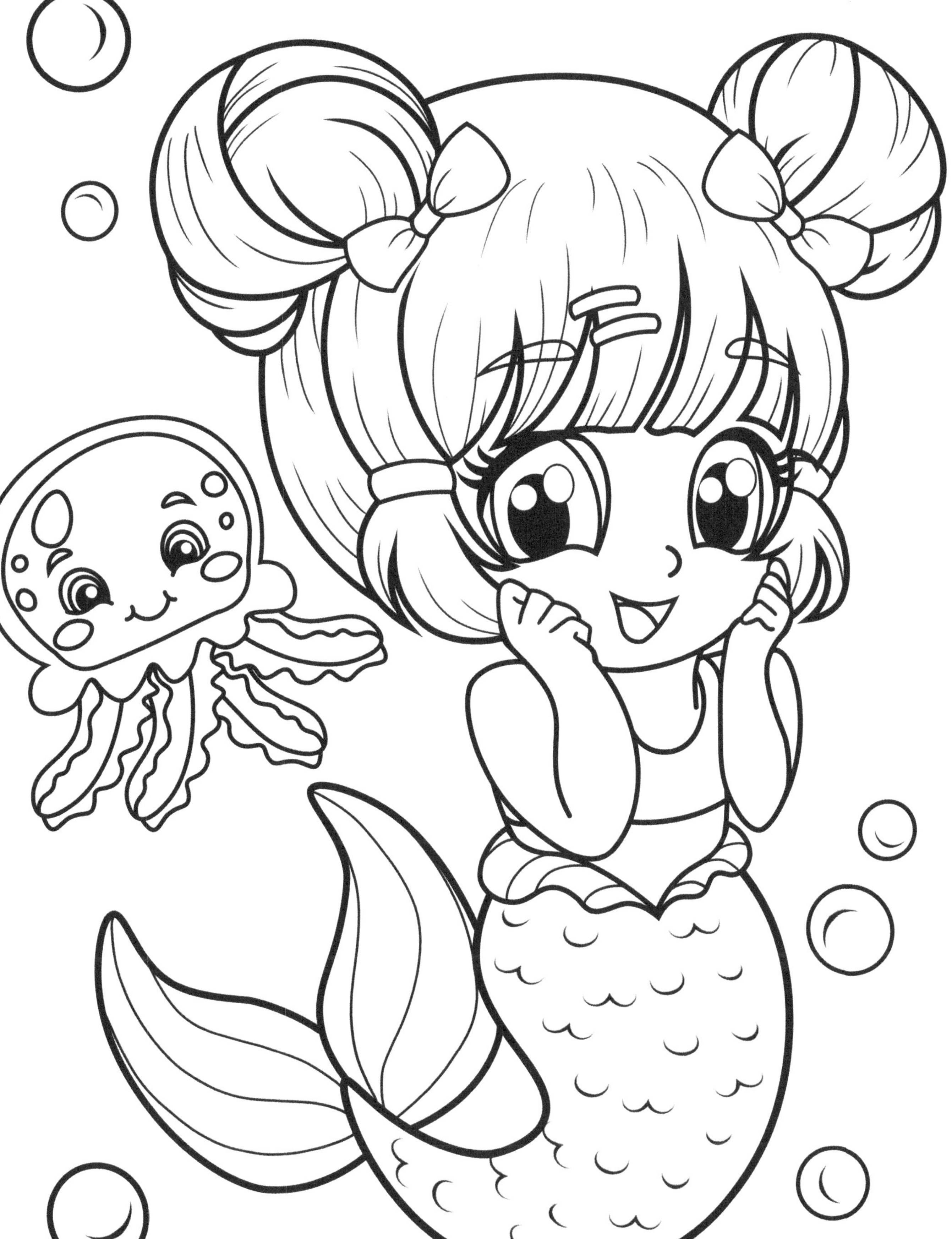

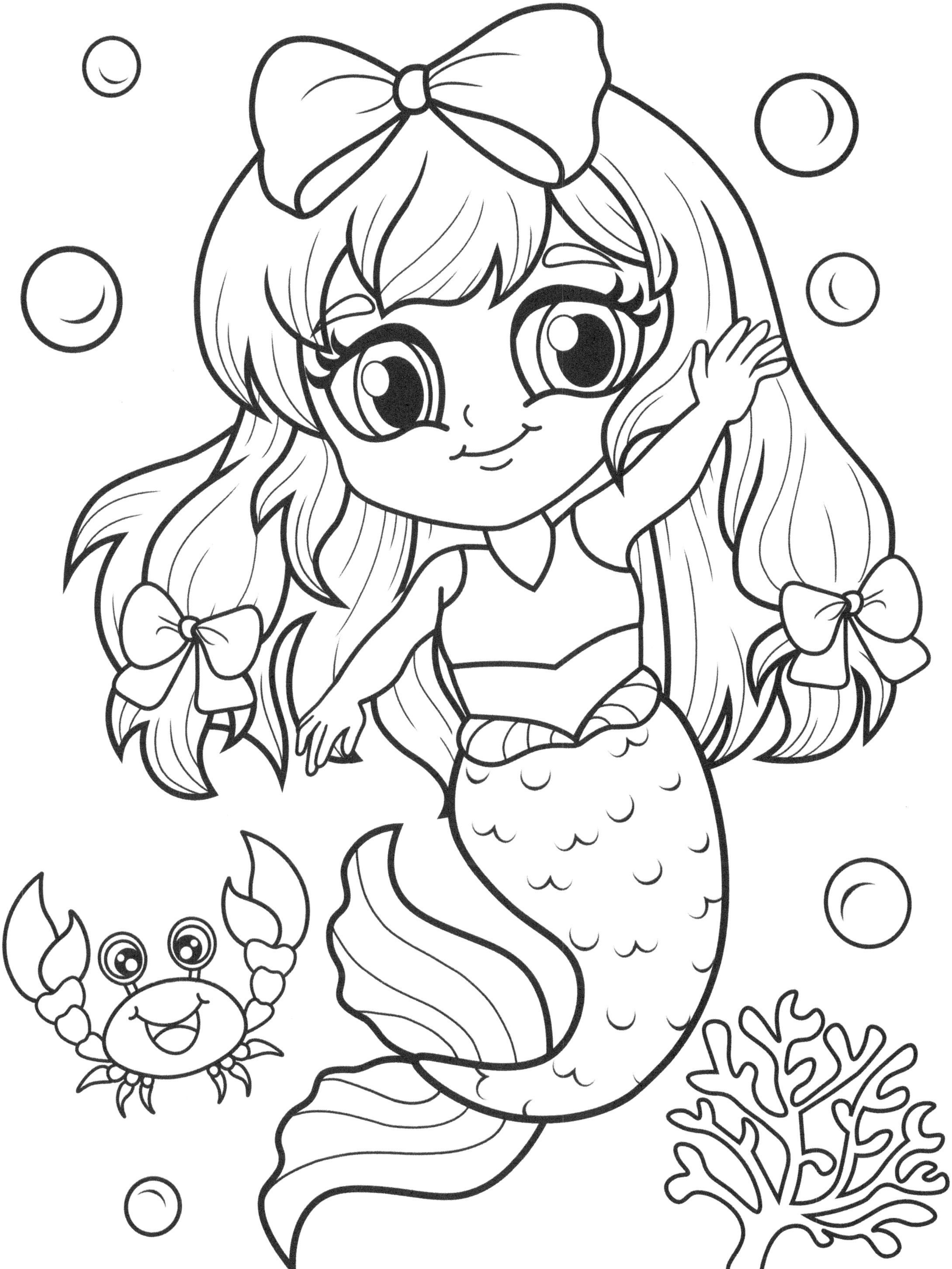

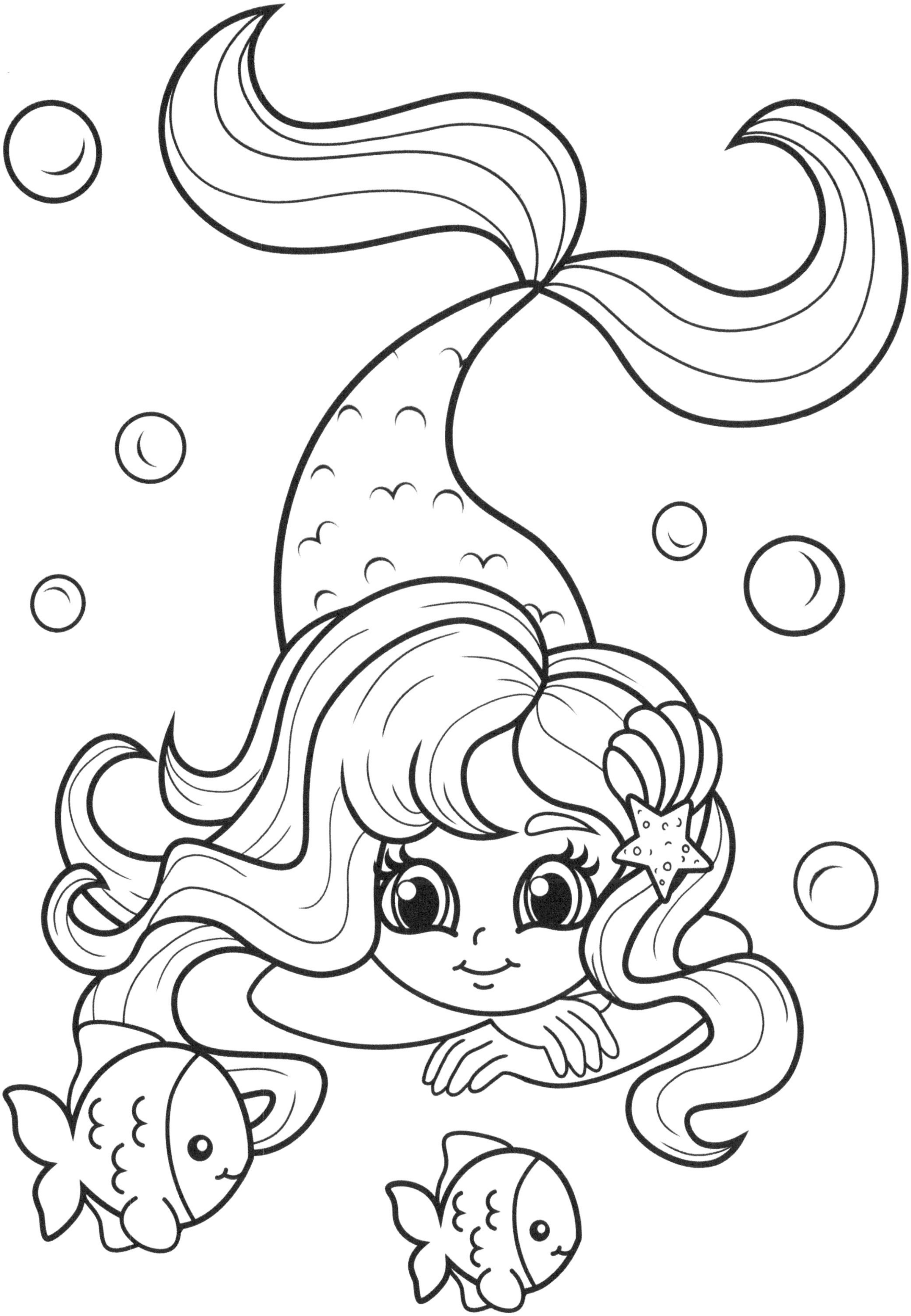

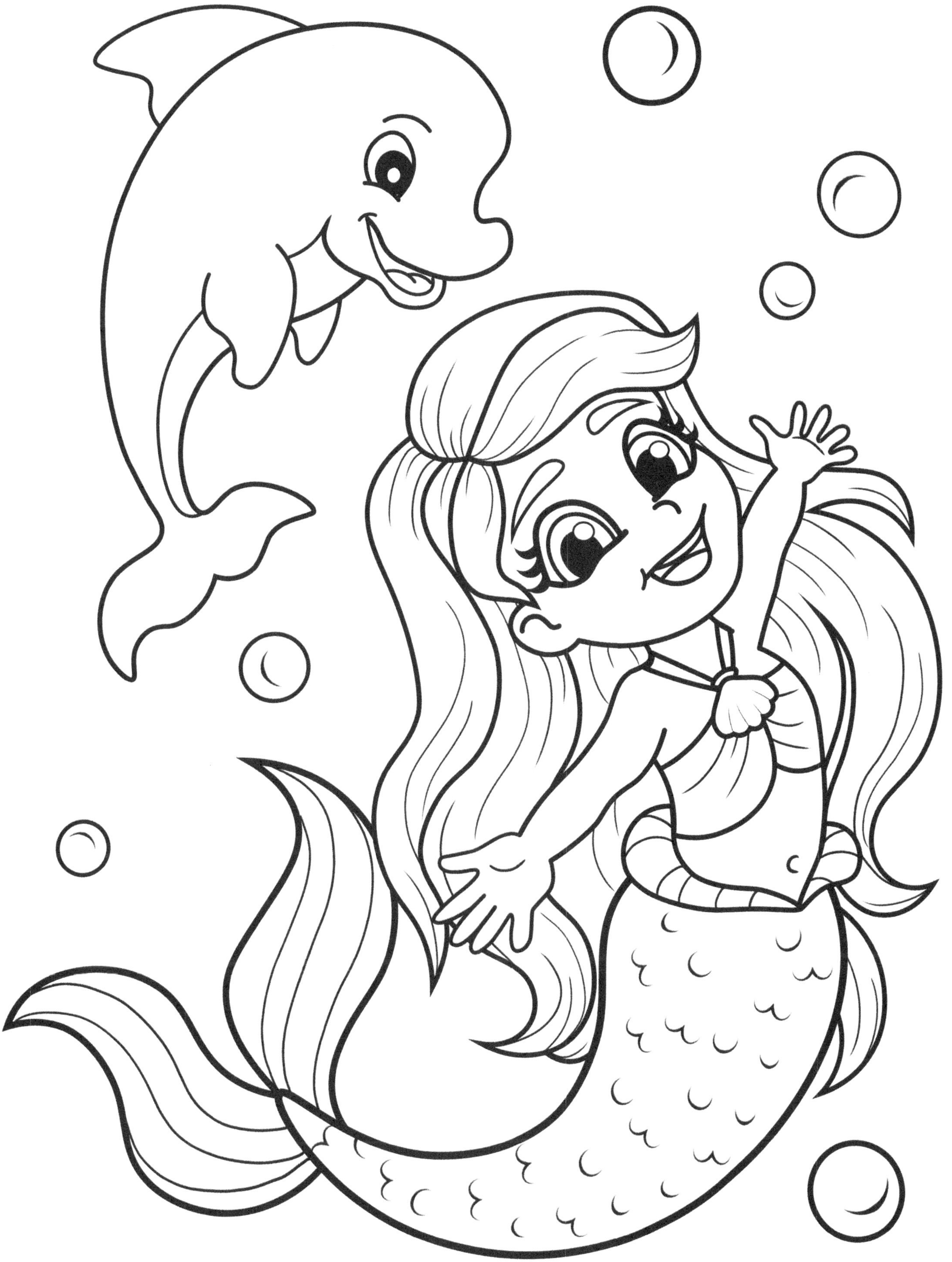

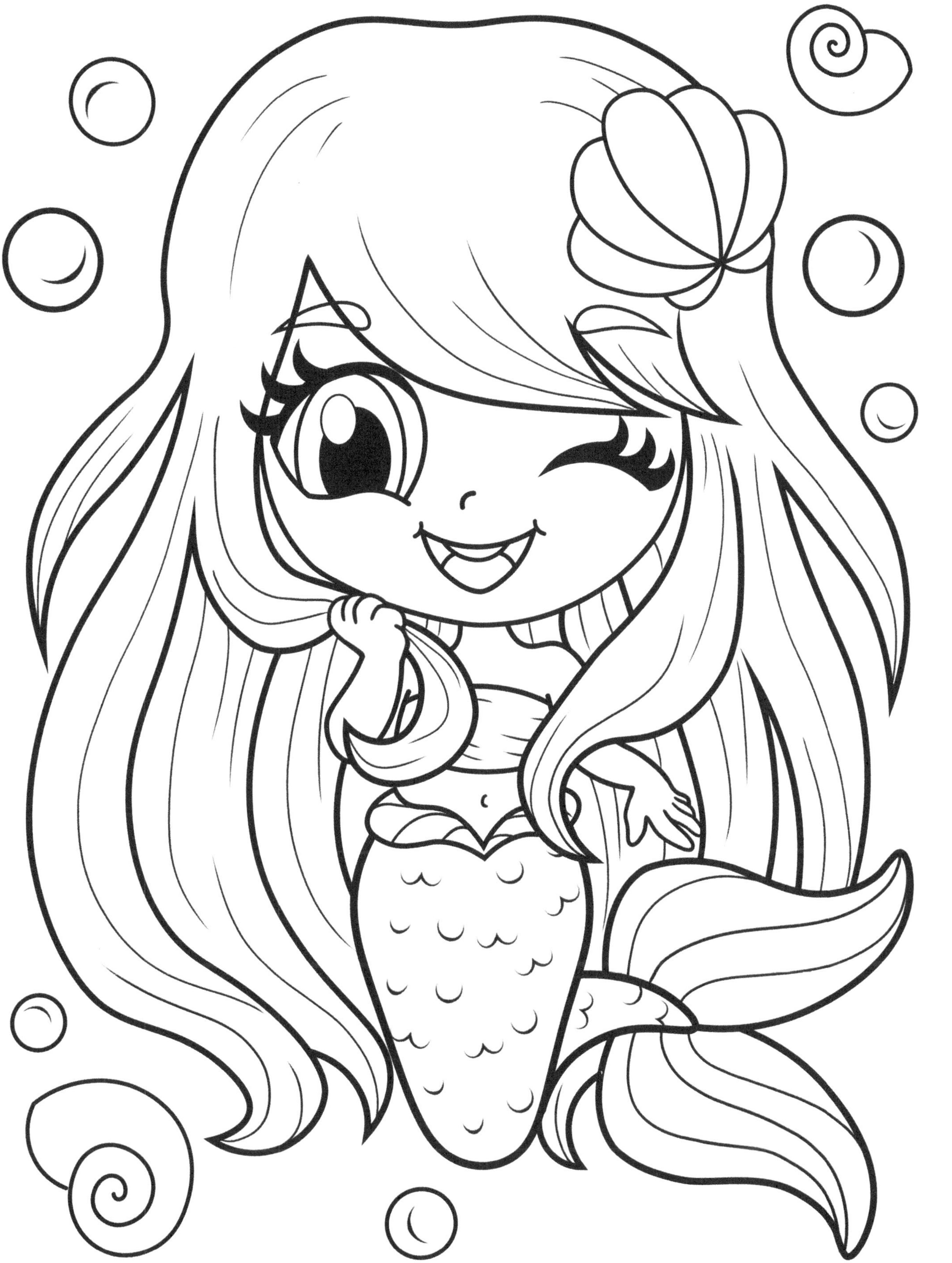

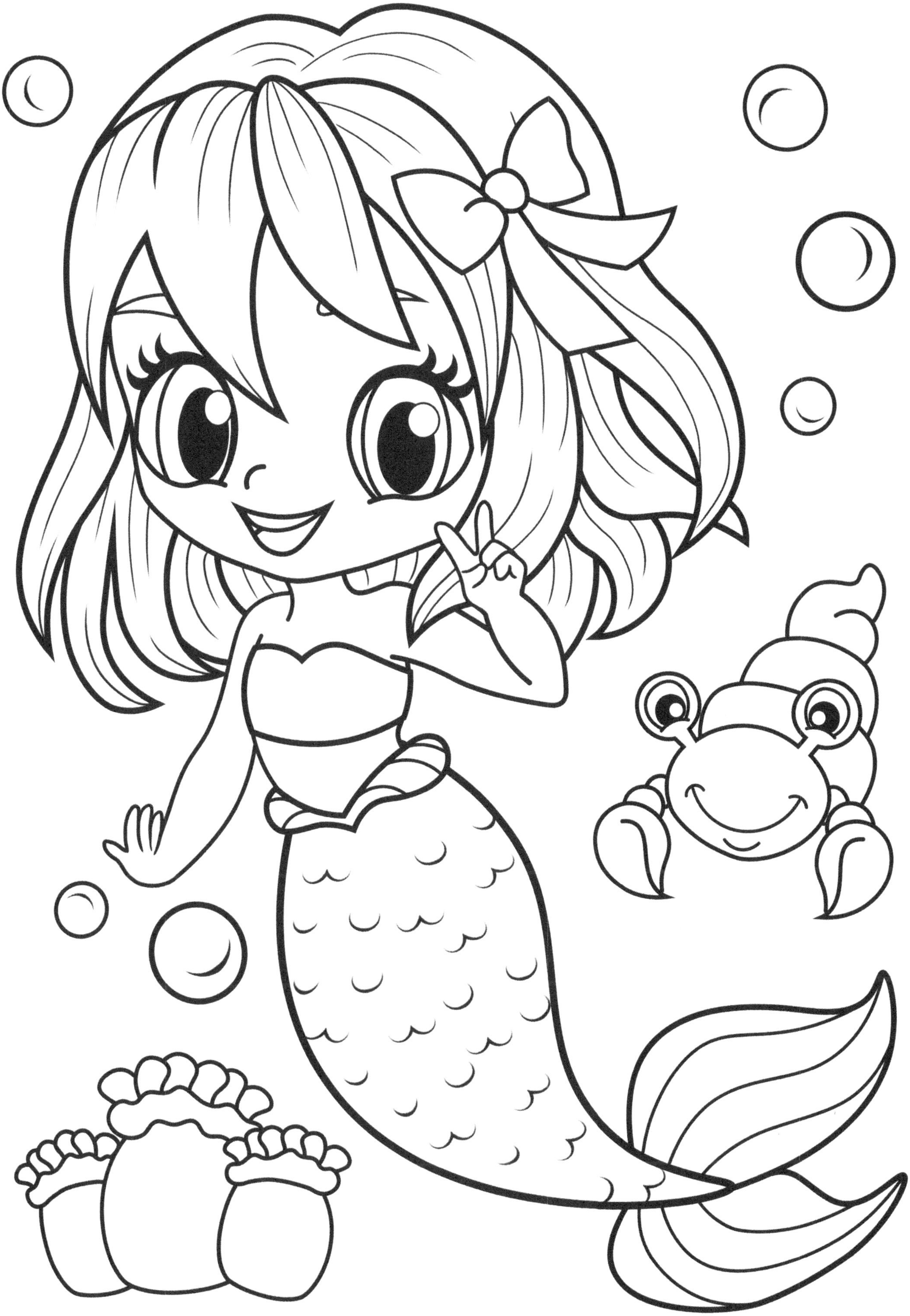

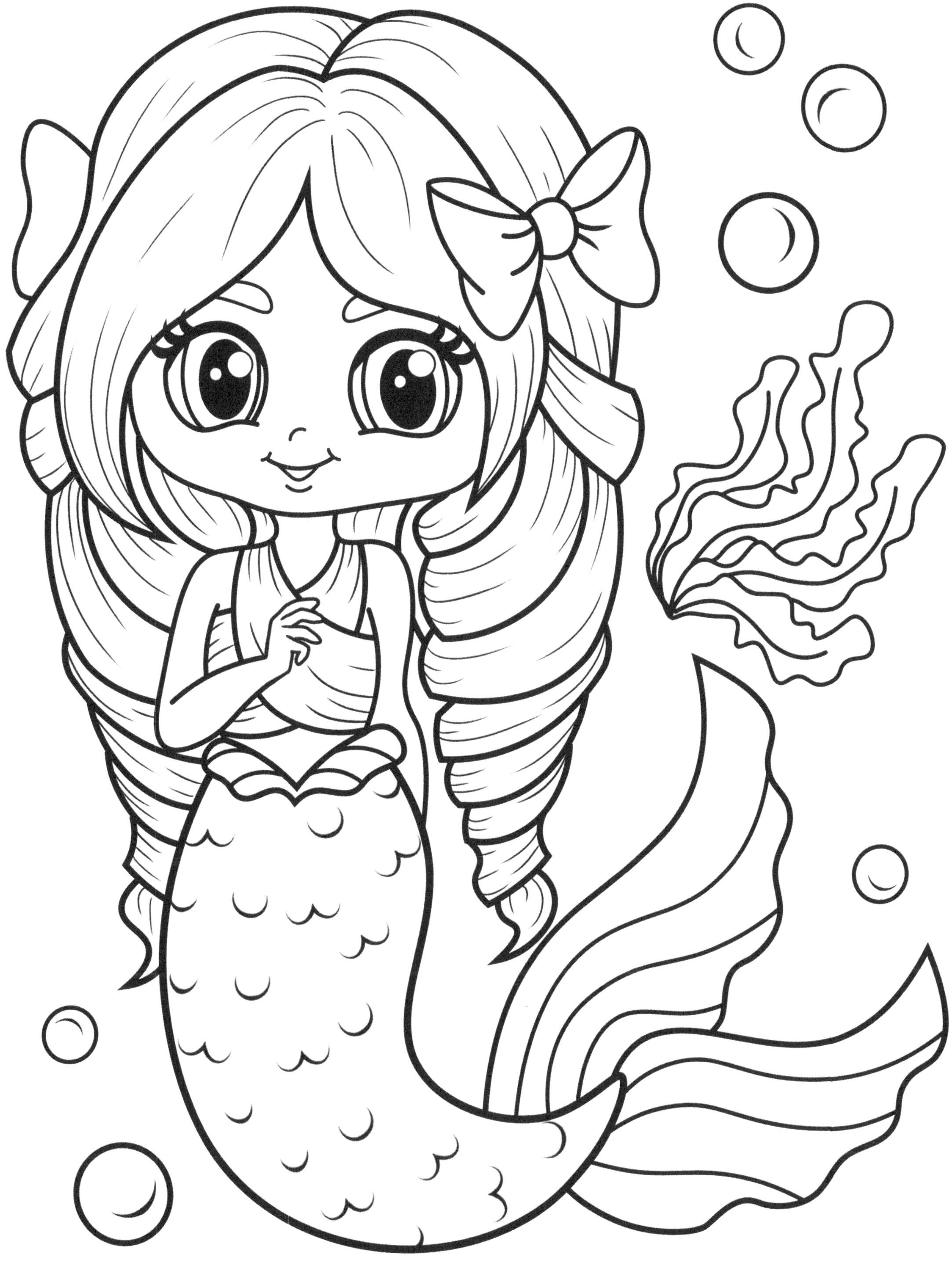

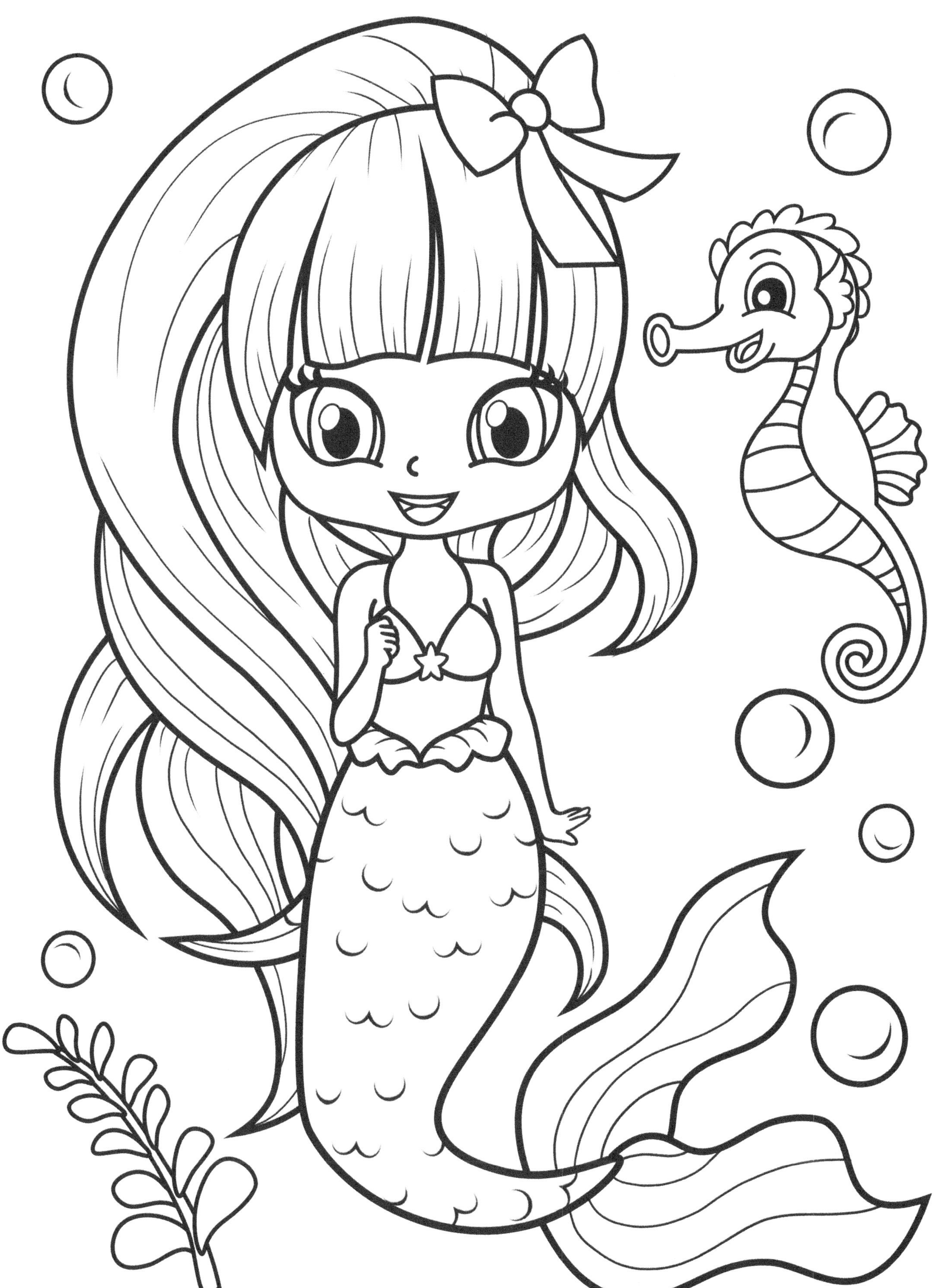

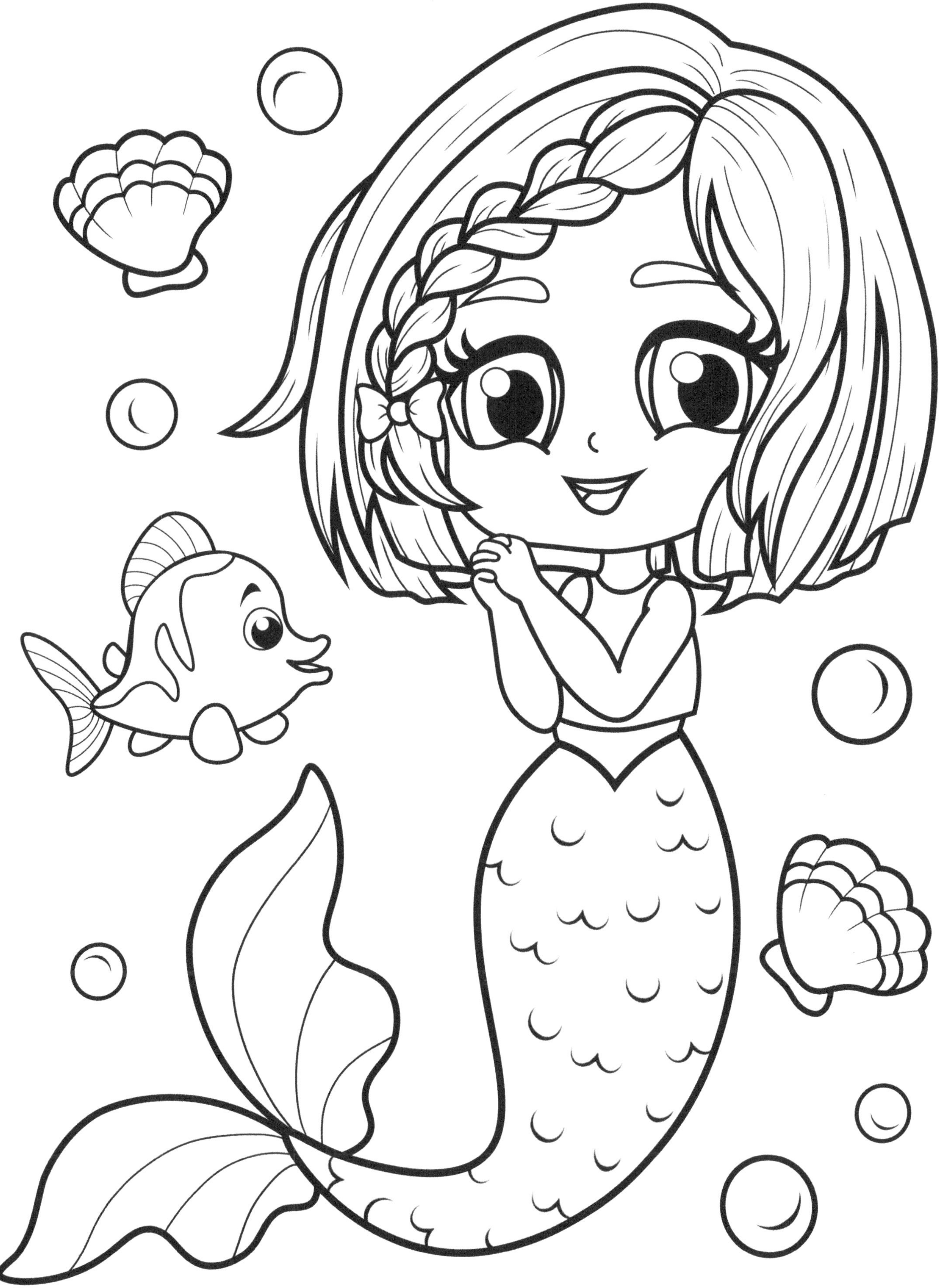

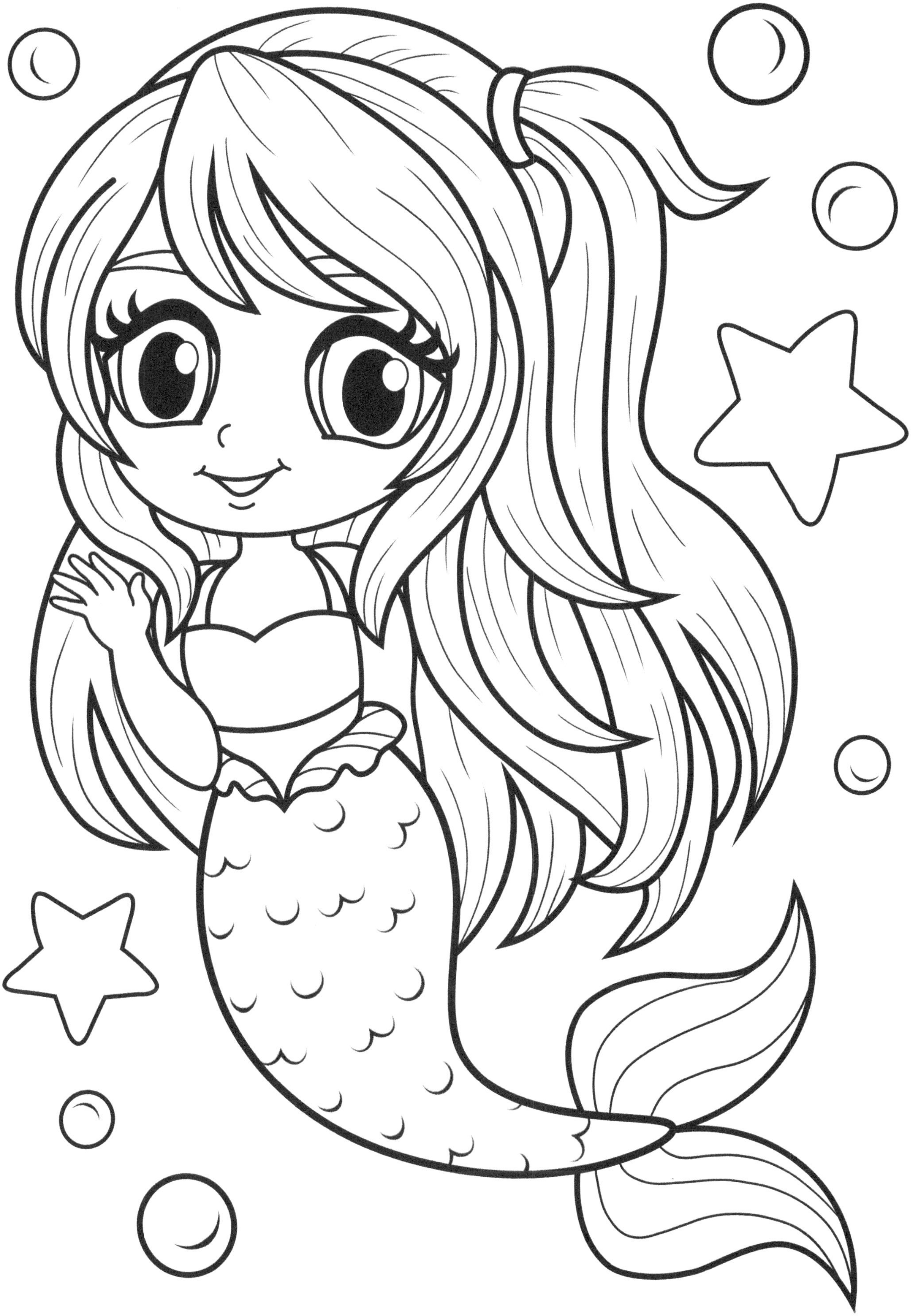

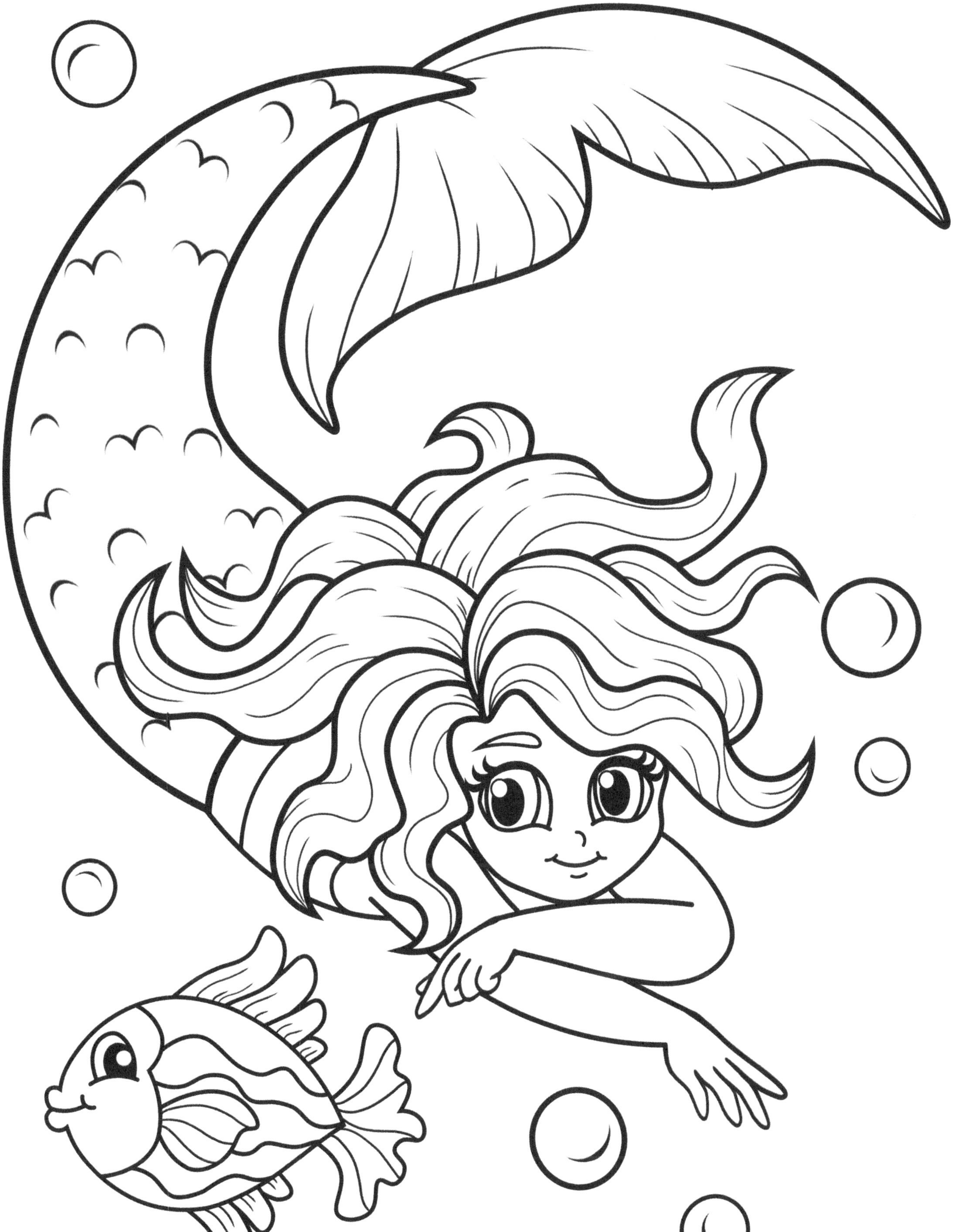

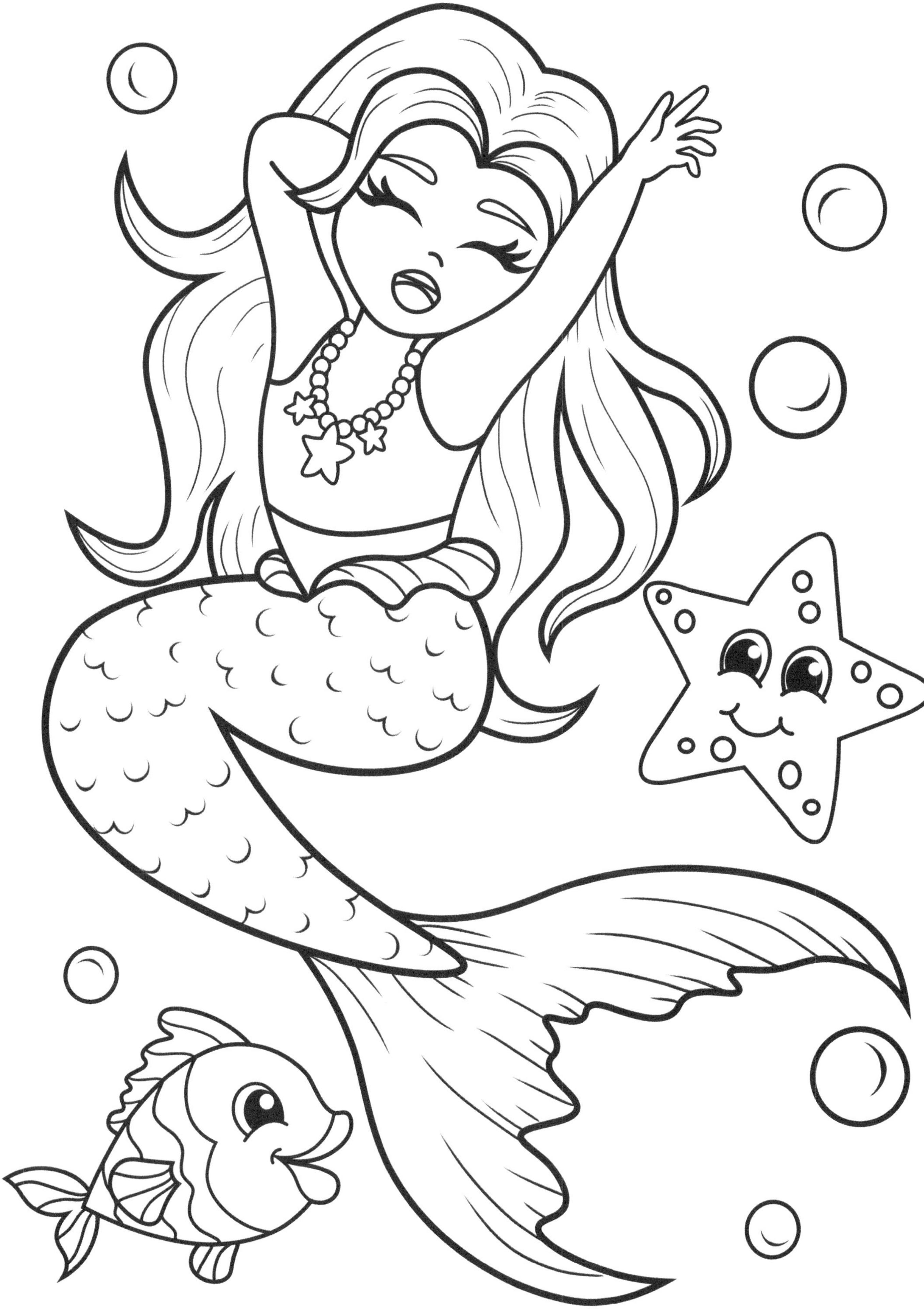

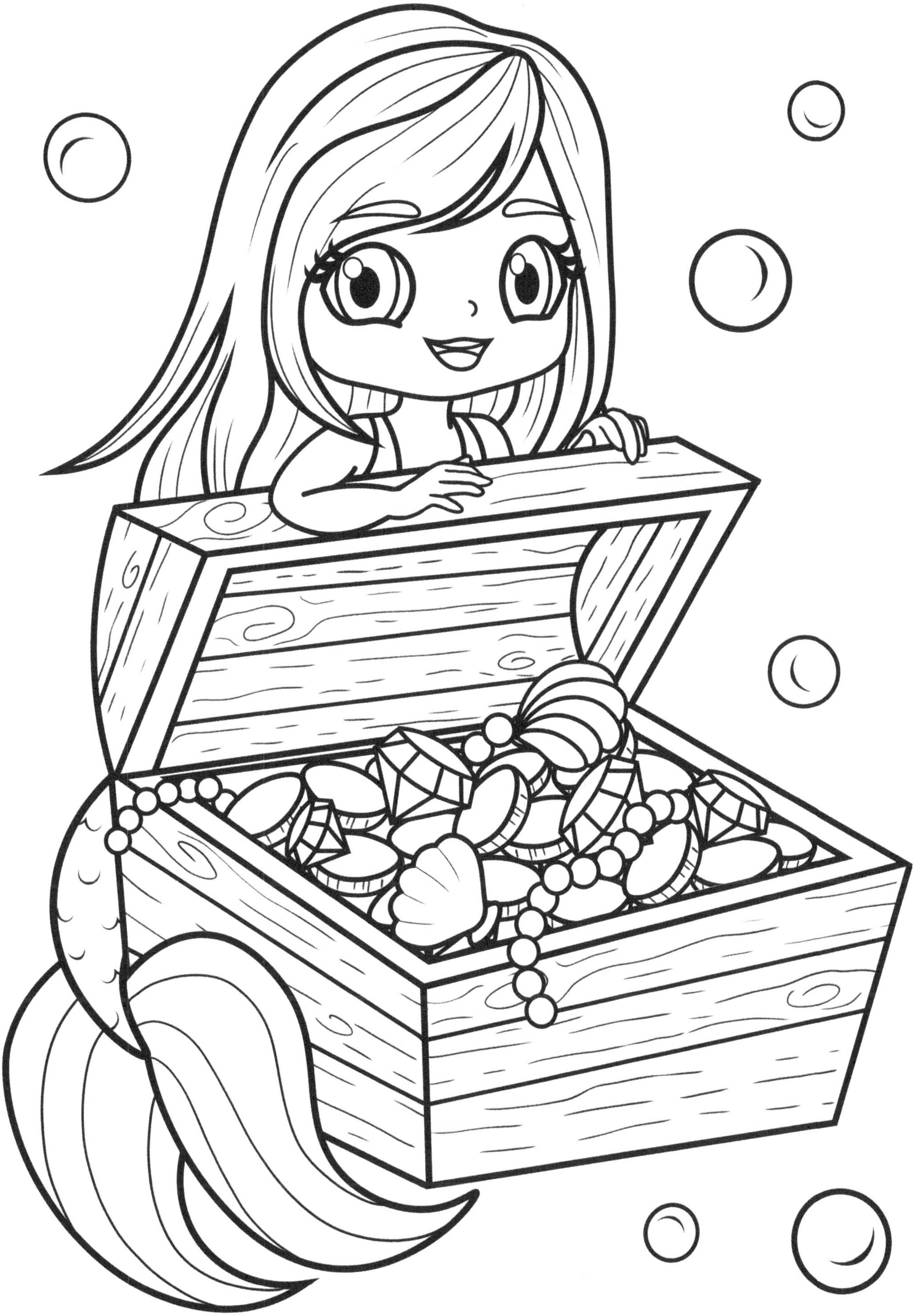

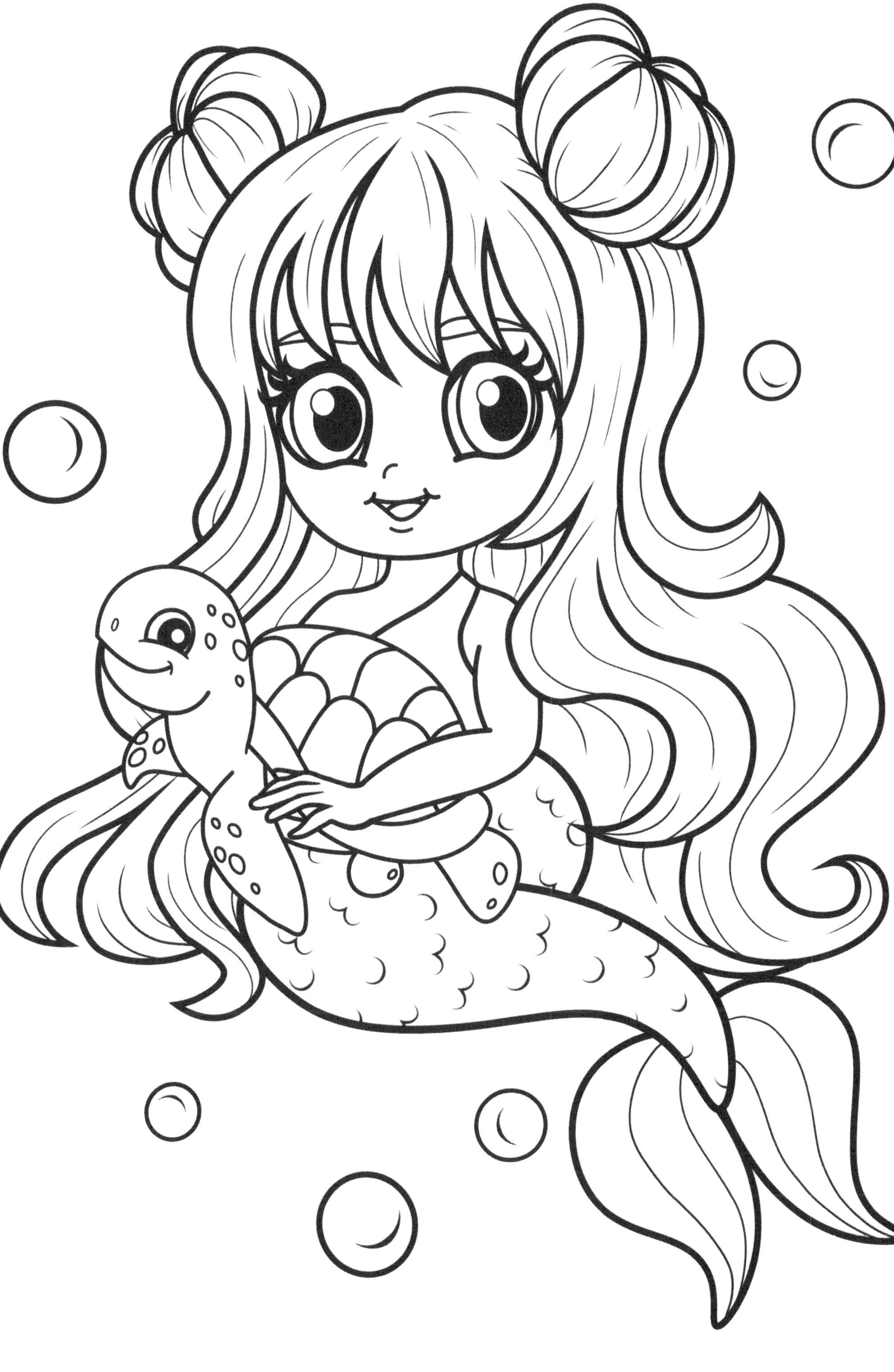

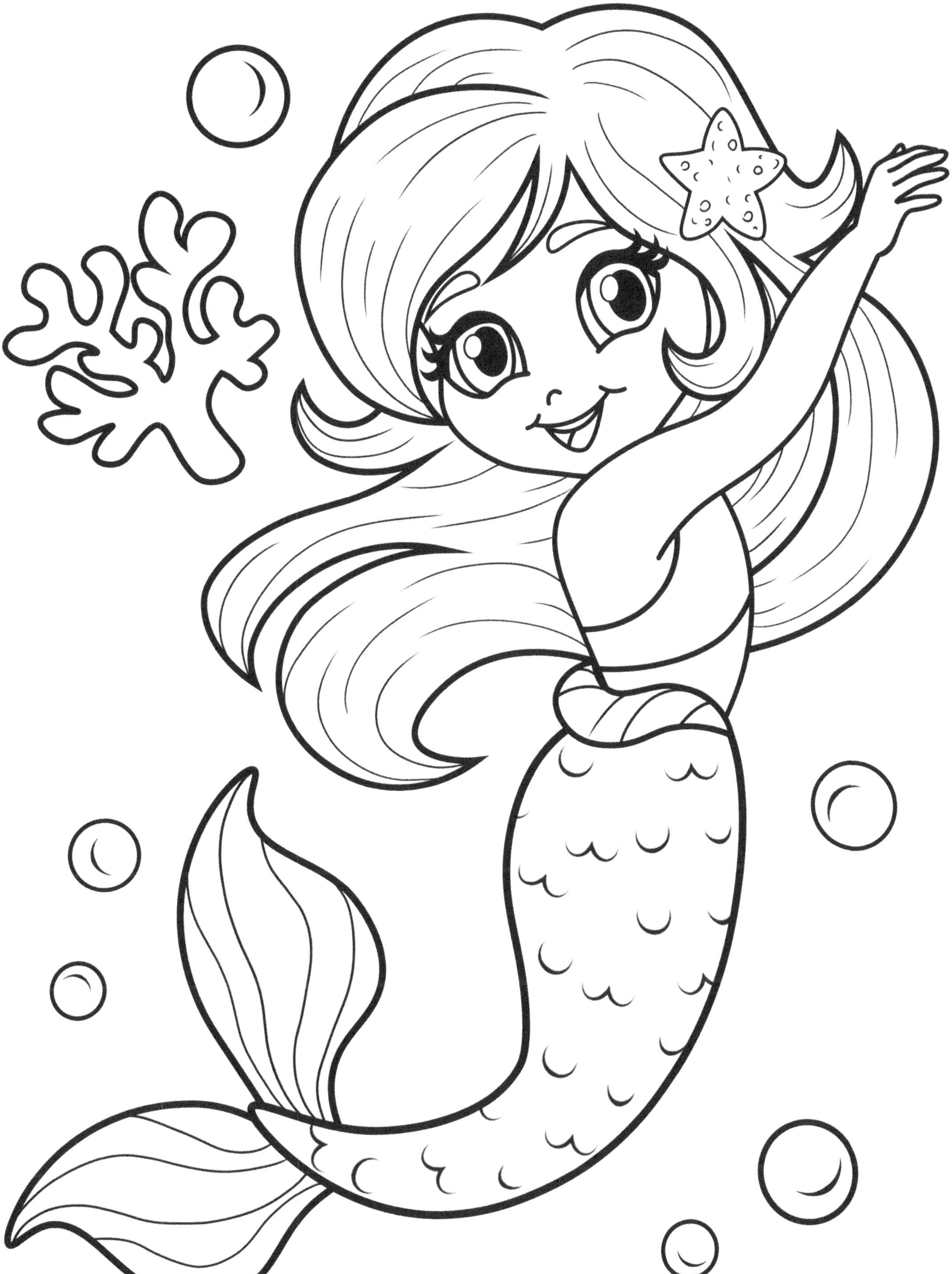

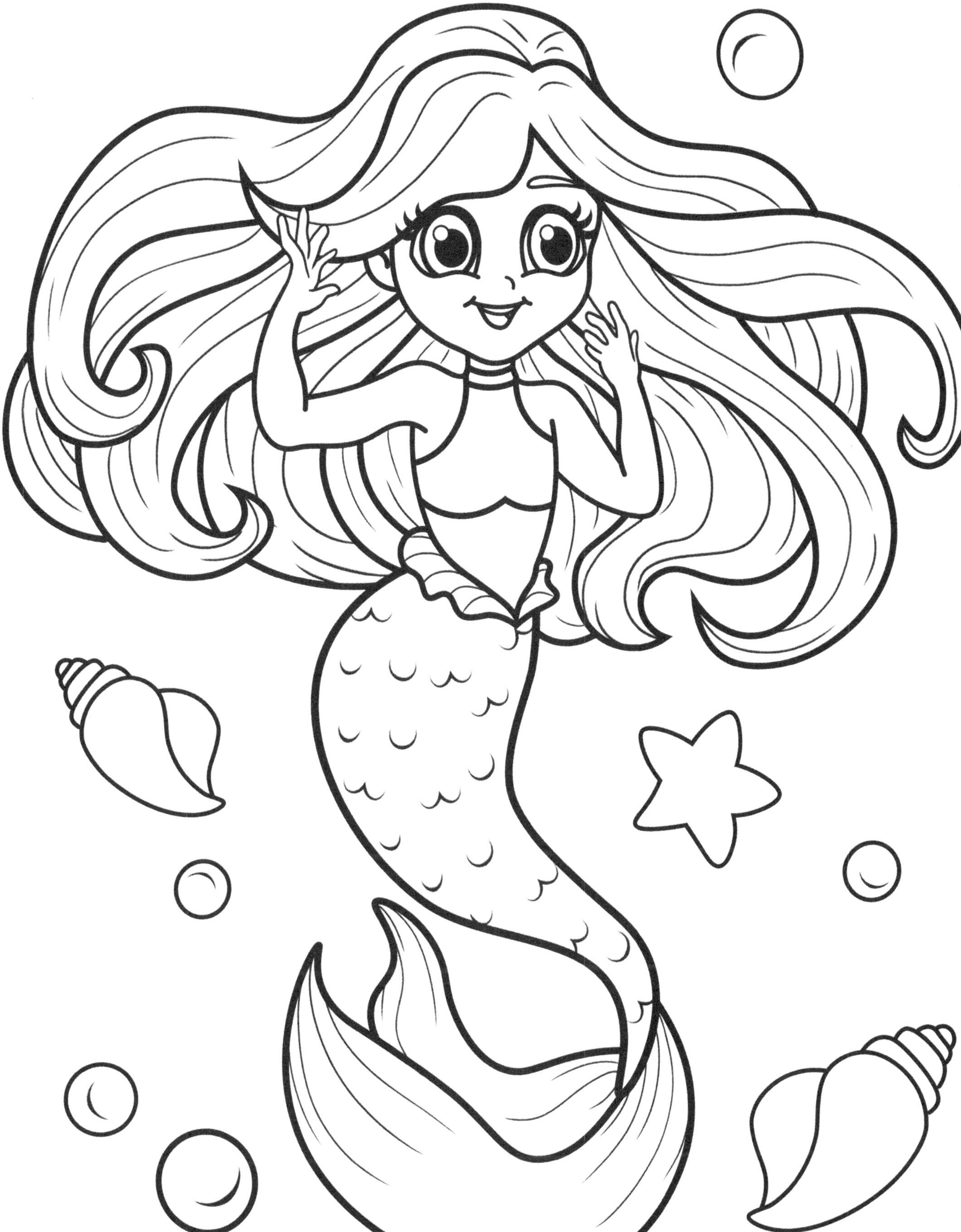

Made in the USA
Las Vegas, NV
11 June 2023

73210955R00057